CW00692537

THE
"NO-NONSENSE" GUIDE
TO
DOING BUSINESS
IN JAPAN

by Jon Woronoff

YOHAN PUBLICATIONS, INC.
Tokyo, Japan

THE
"NO-NONSENSE" GUIDE
TO
DOING BUSINESS
IN JAPAN

A YOHAN LOTUS BOOK / Published 1991

Copyright © 1991 by Jon Woronoff

YOHAN PUBLICATIONS, INC.
14-9 Okubo 3-chome, Shinjuku-ku, Tokyo, Japan

Printed in Japan

Contents

Foreword

What, another book on doing business in Japan! Aren't there enough already? Well, if it is a question of number, then there probably are. If it is a question of usefulness, there may be room for more. In fact, if you take a close look at many of the books on this subject, you could conclude that there is an urgent need for a guide that clears up the nonsense they spread. That, in short, is my intention.

To understand why I wrote this book, it is best to recall my own adventures as a green and gullible businessman in Japan some fifteen years ago. Quite naturally, being new to the market, I read all the guides to doing business in Japan. And, not knowing any better, I believed what they told me. Here was a country full of educated, diligent and loyal workers. The management system brought out the best in them. Companies cooperated for mutual benefit and always thought of the long term. The president's word was as good as a contract. And, if you could provide quality, you were bound to succeed.

Just as naturally, I tried to apply the various tips and strategies these books and similar articles recommended. It was only then that I realized how big the discrepancy was between what the ''experts'' claimed and the realities of doing business in Japan. Each time I did what I was told, it failed or got me in trouble. The more I strove to be a model foreign businessman, the more I was taken for a sucker. It was not until

I chucked the books and figured things out for myself that business improved. I don't think I could express my views of the ''experts'' in printable language at that time.

Yet, even fifteen years later, these and other ''experts'' are still around and they are still peddling much of the same nonsense. The high moral tone of Japanese businessmen. The virtues of the labor force. Quality as the unfailing key to success. And harmony, sweet harmony. Meanwhile, they fail to say a word about things like competition, connections, pricing and profits, as if they were of no consequence.

So, you are still stuck with ''nonsense'' guides. They provide more than enough information on things of marginal significance. They manage to overlook crucial aspects that are incredibly important. And, worst of all, much of their information is mistaken and their advice is misleading. If you were to act on it, you could be in deep trouble, striving for unachievable goals while wasting your true assets. In some cases, it is almost as if they were setting you up for the Japanese.

This means there is a need for a ''no-nonsense'' guide. A guide that provides useful information and leaves the fluff to others. One that exposes the realities of Japanese business rather than spread more illusions. One that offers practical advice but no magic formulas or quick fixes. And one written by someone who actually did business in Japan.

I don't suppose I have fully succeeded. There is probably some information I missed, angles I failed to cover, even advice that may be questionable. But I have done my damnedest to get things right and tell it like it is. In a sense, I have finally written the book I wish I had read when I first arrived. I sincerely hope it helps you in your efforts to make good in Japan.

JON WORONOFF

1

First Things First

Normally, a book—especially a how-to book—should start at the beginning. But that does not happen often with books on how to do business in Japan. They presume a lot of things. One is that every foreigner (*gaijin*) should be enthusiastic about cracking the Japanese market. But there are *gaijin* and *gaijin*. And what may be an excellent idea for some may be a rather poor one for others.

Yet, there you are on page 1, ready to negotiate your big deal with a Japanese company and the author hasn't even bothered telling you how you find a Japanese negotiating partner or how you determine which are the more likely candidates. Or, in other books, you are carefully designing your business card (*meishi*) which is to leave an indelible mark on the Japanese business world, and you don't even know if you should be going to Japan at all.

Well, I think you should start a bit earlier than that. You should begin with the essential, difficult and trying question of whether *you* (and not some fictionalized, standardized *gaijin*) should be doing business in Japan. This is a good idea for some companies. It is an absolutely lousy one for others. And you should not be printing your *meishi* until you come to a rational decision.

While not easy to make, that decision must have some appeal or it would not have attracted so many foreign companies (*gaishikei kigyo* or *gaishi* for short). Just how many is hard to know exactly. Still, according to one estimate, there were recently some 1,300 foreign wholly owned subsidiaries, 1,400 foreign branches and 1,600 foreign-Japanese joint ventures.[1] To this may be added hundreds of companies established under Japanese law by foreigners living in Japan, thousands of companies licensing products, franchising services or transferring technologies and tens of thousands exporting one article or another.

Why did they come? That is what we will look at now.

Why Go To Japan?

The general case for doing business in Japan is so well known, and inherently so convincing, that there is no need to belabor it. Thus, I will just highlight some of the more significant aspects. You can get much more in pep talks in the media or local chambers of commerce.

First of all, the Japanese market is large. It is very large. In fact, it is the second biggest in the world with Japan's consumer spending ranking second to the United States and per capita consumer spending, once converted into dollars, almost comparable. If you like round figures, you might mull over the fact that its gross national product is now about $3 trillion.

The market has grown this big, among other things, because Japan already has a population of some 125 million people, which is about half the size of the United States but more than twice that of larger European countries. They are crammed together in a relatively small space, only about as big as California, which makes the market exceptionally compact and easier to service in certain ways. The population is not increasing much nowadays, but the composition is shifting from many young to more old.

By the way, the Japanese are not just any people. They are people whose earnings have grown steadily to the point where the per capita income is already higher than in the United States and much of Europe and only lags some oil kingdoms and Scandinavia. Meanwhile, in addition to income earned regularly by the sweat of their brow, many Japanese have suddenly become richer due to soaring property or stock prices and a fair number have inherited appreciable wealth.

The Japanese are known to be "frugal." That is a traditional virtue, or so they say. Well, while this is not generally noticed, there has been a tendency for many to become less so. The savings rate is still very high. But the debt level is growing faster as younger (and older) Japanese become accustomed to credit cards and the like. This means that spending has actually outpaced earnings and the pent-up demand makes the market even more attractive than otherwise.

Not only is this a big market, it is an expanding market. That is because the economy has continued growing at a faster pace than other advanced countries, if not quite the rates it achieved in the 1950s and 1960s. This is making the population more affluent, enhancing their purchasing power, and allowing them to absorb more goods and services than before. At the same time, the value of the yen has continued growing so that purchasing power in dollar terms races ahead.

This means that certain sectors are growing at uncommonly fast rates, especially those that were neglected before. They include consumer goods, from ordinary to luxuries. There is still a demand for high tech products and the technology to produce them. With a shift in demographics toward more old people, there is a burgeoning market for anything sought by seniors, from clothing to medicine. But the biggest growth is in services, whether fast food, leisure, health care or financial.

Finally, the Japanese are under pressure to import more. For decades, the economy has been export-led, selling more than it bought. That sort of behavior naturally did not appeal to its trading partners which have pressured Japan to buy more from them. Since imports are presently at a comparatively low level, changing economic circumstances plus political pressure are opening the market like never before. This makes the present a considerably better time to do business in Japan than the past ever was.

But, Should *You* Go?

Fine, Japan is a great market! It did not take much to convince you. In fact, you probably already knew it. But this still doesn't answer the more pertinent question of whether this is a great market for you.

Such a question cannot be answered in the abstract. That much is obvious, although many foreigners try to crack the market without even bothering to consider it. For it is necessary at this point to disaggregate. You are not just any seller. You have a specific product, of a specific quality, sold at a specific price, targeted at a specific segment, and so on. No matter what might be expected for any number of other products, you still have to ascertain whether yours will make the grade.

This implies that, as a first step, you should at least check on how your product will presumably fare. You have to see what the competing products are, if any. You have to see how yours compares. You have to determine whether the consumers are likely to be receptive. And you have to figure out the costs of marketing it so you know whether you can earn a reasonable return.

In so doing, you should remember that Japanese consumers may be considerably more demanding than your own. So, you must check whether the quality is good enough. You must be able to assure prompt and reliable delivery, otherwise Japanese distributors or manufacturers will not want to deal with you given their own imperatives. You must look into the aspect of service more closely, since the Japanese tend to be unusually fastidious about this. Further details are included in Chapter 8.

I'm certain you have heard all that before. The Japanese want quality, quality, quality, plus delivery, delivery, delivery, plus service, service, service. So do make an effort to provide that.

But don't forget about another aspect which most books on doing business in Japan overlook. That is price. I have rarely read that goods can make it on the basis of price. Perhaps that is because so much emphasis is placed on quality, delivery, service, etc. But price is playing an increasingly important role. That is because fairly recent social and economic phenomena are affecting the market in many ways. In a nutshell, there is a growing schism between the top and the bottom.[2]

For the first time, there are truly "rich" people, or at least people who possess plenty of money which they tend to spend with unaccustomed abandon. This includes those who have made a fortune on property or the stock market, those who have inherited wealth, or those who are just passing through a period when spending is the vogue. This latter involves especially young women (sometimes also men) who have a job but still live at home and can therefore spend nearly all their earnings on the good life. They are known as the "bachelor aristocrats" and they fuel the consumer boom.

At the other end are many who have become relatively (or absolutely) poorer. They include people who must pay more than they can afford for housing, who have lost their job or merely retired and find it hard to get by on a pension or social security and, quite often, the parents of the "bachelor aristocrats" who have earnings that barely cover expenses. For the latter, the split may be personal: they spend more than they should on articles that are seen in public in order to maintain "face"; they consequently spend less on the rest.

This may imply spending more on luxuries and less on necessities, more on a Dior scarf and less on underwear, more on whiskey and less on tea.

Obviously, for many consumer articles and fashionable luxuries, price is almost no consideration. That means business is booming for Gucci, Dior and Remy Martin. This aspect is already well documented. Less known is that business is picking up notably for quite ordinary producers of quite ordinary articles. Many Korean, Taiwan, Hong Kong and other firms are now busily selling cheap watches, garments, household appliances, consumer electronics and so on. They are avidly sought by those in Japan who cannot afford anything else, a less noble but no less interesting clientele that should also keep growing.

By the way, I mentioned that you should check whether your product looks promising. I did not mean product in the restricted sense of a manufactured good. It could just as well be a service. The service sector is increasingly the most attractive for foreign companies. While the Japanese have done an excellent job of manufacturing, they have only been so-so when it comes to modern services. For many, foreigners have more expertise and experience and could compete even more effectively than for manufactures.

So, check whether your product *or service* has what it takes to make it in Japan. But, even if it does not, you may still want to go. There is one last reason. And it may be the clincher.

With Japanese firms expanding aggressively overseas, whether through exports or investments, you will want to know what they are up to. You might do well to have a small office in Tokyo which would try to sell your product (or service) just to see how it fares. Meanwhile, it could also look into what your competitors are doing, whether they have come out with improved products or are expanding production. You may even get advance warning on how to react if the Japanese are preparing an export offensive. I think this is called a "listening post," but it could more correctly be assimilated to a spy operation.

Don't Let Them Scare You Off!

I would think that it is hard enough to make the decision of whether to go ahead without having to contend with all sorts of spurious reasons to hold back. There are ideas, arguments, rumors which are sometimes spread by quite reputable sources and intimate that, if one does not do something truly extraordinary, Japan is no place to be. I think they may be inspired by the Japanese, who don't want new competitors to begin with. Or they derive from the foreign mystique of how hard it is to do business in Japan. Whatever the case, they are unnecessary hindrances.

First of all, the notion that your product or service must be "unique" to succeed. Even the U.S. Department of Commerce foolishly insisted that retailers must be sure to offer "a unique product mix or service concept."[3] I never saw this mentioned in books on how to do business in America, or Europe, or China. Only for Japan is uniqueness a supposed requirement.

Well, how in this competitive world where everybody knows what everybody else is doing can you come up with "unique" products? Come to think of it, how many "unique" products are there around? How many products do something that no others do and are protected by patents or proprietary rights? And how many companies have access to such products?

If you look at what Japan imports, the bulk of it is hardly unique. Yes, there is a big place for brand name and high fashion articles, many high tech products are sophisticated (if not quite unique), and there are patented pharmaceuticals, etc. But most of the stuff if quite ordinary, whether processed raw materials and foods, consumer articles, capital goods or services (banking, insurance, leisure, etc.). The further downmarket you go, the more ordinary it gets, with Taiwan's Tatung making a mint by selling electric fans!

No, even for Japan, you do not need something unique. But you should have something that is somewhat superior (or at least different). That can be in quality, design, convenience, service . . . or price. You can sell the most ordinary of goods in the right sector if they are cheap enough. That is why exports from the nearby Asian countries, those which are stuck at the bottom of the market, are growing faster than those of more advanced countries which actually do have pretty special items.

So, the second mistaken reason not to try Japan is the concept that quality, delivery and service are all that count and, if you cannot compare, forget Japan. They are important. They are terribly important. But they are not the only things that matter. You can be somewhat below par there and compensate with price. This means that comparative advantage, the same principle that governs trade everywhere else, also applies in Japan. Don't let them tell you otherwise!

Another must, according to the pundits, is commitment. You must be willing to put more up front in Japan, to wait for a longer time to penetrate the market, to wait yet longer to make a return on your investment, and to wait much more to be a true success. I don't disagree on the principle. But I question the details.

Obviously, you need commitment. Japan is a tough market. But that does not imply a massive effort. You can start off small and grow. That may be better than making too big a splash and finding you cannot meet your own expectations or those aroused in the marketplace. In addition, there are easier ways of entering, ones which require less commitment than a big wholly owned operation, such as a joint venture or merely exporting or licensing. For more on this, read Chapter 4.

(By the way, I am not even convinced that the commitment always has to be that exceptional. If you do your homework carefully, if you pick the right product or service, and market it in the right way, you may not have to wait so long for a decent return. Certainly not the three-to-five years that are presently quoted as the necessary gestation period.)

Many foreigners feel that, since Japan has so many "big" companies, it is impossible to succeed if you are not "big." That is also a spurious worry. True, it does not hurt to be big, to have many products, lots of personnel and plenty of financial resources. But that is only decisive if your Japanese rivals are equally big or bigger. If you look more closely, you may find that your direct competitors are fairly small, maybe even smaller than you. In fact, there is an amazing number of small operations, often set up by a single foreigner (plus a Japanese spouse in some cases), that made a go of it. There are also countless small companies that discovered just the right niche and are prospering.[4]

One other misconception, which is never openly expressed, is racial. Virtually all of the literature on doing business in Japan implicitly assumes that the companies are Western. After all, you want a unique product, you need great experience, you require enormous financial clout and it is good if you are in high tech. Who meets those qualifications? The big Western multinationals. But, as noted, there is ever more room in other sectors which make none of these demands and where price is an essential factor. That surely signifies that there is room for companies from developing countries, especially the nearby Asian "newly industrialized countries."

Finally, sexual discrimination . . . in the literature and in Japan. True, the Japanese do not think very highly of the business acumen of women. Indeed, if they suspected a businesswoman were competent, it might repel them more than attract them. Foreign businessmen also seem to think that only a tough macho approach will work. Still, many foreign women have managed to set up and run their own companies, although they rarely appear on the staffs of the foreign multinationals. Be that as it may, they face more hurdles than men and, in practice, most of the participants in the business world are men, especially on the Japanese side.

Still Tough, But Less So

The purpose of this chapter is not to talk you into doing business but to explain, as well as I can, what the advantages and drawbacks are. While indicating that many obstacles are not as serious or valid as thought, I would not like to imply that Japan is an easy market. It is not. It is a tough market. It is damn tough.

First of all, you have to face competition which is more intense than what you are familiar with back home, no matter where that may be. Japanese companies compete with one another more aggressively than do American, or German, or even Korean companies. That is because much of the competition is based on market share, a much harsher task master than mere profit.

Liberal market economies have a win-win ethos. You try to boost profits by increasing the margin, something which does not necessarily upset your competitors. In fact, it allows them to raise margins and boost profits as well. Admittedly, in hard times there is pressure, and you would bring down prices, obliging others to do the same. But you would not want to lower them so far as to endanger profits under ordinary circumstances. Price-cutting and competitive wars are more the exception.

In Japan, they are almost the rule because you must undercut your competitors to increase market share. This is a very serious matter since now you are in a win-lose situation. If you gain market share, somebody must lose, because there are only 100%. This leaves foreign companies in a bind when competing with Japanese rivals, for they would not want to lower prices enough to hurt the bottom line. Yet, if they do not fight back, they will gradually lose market share no matter how fine profits are. The end result could be that they are driven out of the market.

In addition, you will be coping with unusually demanding customers. These may be ordinary consumers, men and women who want the best in quality, service, etc. and will be almost fastidious in their selection. You will not get off any easier if you sell to Japanese companies. They are strict in their demands of quality, delivery, service and price. You have probably already heard this before, so there is no need to expand on it now.

These are "natural" barriers, in the sense of arising spontaneously in the market and not being man-made. There are also lots of artificial barriers blocking access to Japan. No matter how often or how earnestly Japanese politicians, bureaucrats and businessmen insist that Japan is one of the world's most open markets, that is not quite true. The Japanese have demonstrated great ingenuity in devising obstacles to keep out imported goods. To learn more about them, you should read *Unlocking Japan's Markets*.[5]

The good thing is that these barriers are decreasing. Tariff levels have declined considerably. Indeed, by now the average rate is lower than in most industrialized countries, although you may encounter peaks in certain sectors. Quotas are disappearing aside from some foodstuffs and leather goods. Nontariff barriers do remain. The Japanese have eliminated hundreds of NTBs, but they did not get rid of all of them. Moreover, when nobody is looking, they try to create new ones. Still, even these are not insurmountable.

What does pose a serious problem even now are the tight relations that exist between Japanese companies. This can be the reputed warm and friendly relations that derive from cooperating with one another for decades. Or it can involve harder, more resistant links resulting from financial control, shareholding, domination of retailing, etc. This is typified by the groups or *keiretsu* which will be dealt with in more detail in the next chapter.

Fortunately, no matter how irritating or inhibiting, these assorted barriers are—on the whole—receding and it is getting easier to penetrate the market. Not only that, the Japanese government has been shamed into actually promoting imports. It has taken various steps which redound to the advantage of foreign companies. Among other things, it urges Japanese manufacturers to procure more parts or equipment abroad, it suggests that individual consumers buy more imported goods, and it organizes special "buy foreign" campaigns. In addition, specialized bodies promote import missions and trade fairs and undertake other activities to help foreigners enter the market. Certainly, this effort has been less fruitful than the earlier export drives, but it has created a much more congenial environment.

Still, don't expect the Japanese to take you by the hand (unless they have to meet their "quota" of imported goods). If you want to make it in Japan, you must do the right things in the right ways. You have to figure out how to get around the barriers and live with the business structure and cultural hangups. This will be discussed in subsequent chapters.

What To Do Before You Go

Once you have decided to tackle the Japanese market, you should prepare. Obviously according to all the manuals, the first thing to do is print up some *meishi*. These are the Japanese version of business cards which are distributed profusely and you may well need hundreds. They should be bilingual, your language plus Japanese. That is, assuming your language is an alphabet or character one readily grasped by the Japanese. Otherwise, and even for some European languages, perhaps English would be the better second language.

Meishi can often be made in your home country by local translation companies or major airlines, especially Japanese carriers. But just hope and pray that the translation is correct. Otherwise you may end up a laughing stock. Just in case, bring along some of your old cards. The alternative is to have them made in Japan. The turnaround is fast, the price is high, but there is still no guarantee of quality. Not even in Japan!

As all intelligent businessmen should realize, you don't just plunk your *meishi* on the table. You hand it formally to your counterparts, making a bow of 15%. You collect theirs and inspect them earnestly. You do not dump them unceremoniously in your pocket or deal them out like a deck of cards on the table. What's that? How do you know your bow is the regulation 15%. Academics are so remiss in details of this nature. I assume you can draw a line on your office wall and practice every day.

You should also get a foretaste of Japan and things Japanese, according to certain authors. Yes, why not go out for a good Japanese dinner? Try the *sushi,* it provides excellent practice to learn the art of wielding chopsticks and is served at most receptions. You may not like the octopus, but that can be forgiven a *gaijin.* Also get in some drinking practice. It is amazing how much useful information can be obtained over a glass of whisky. No, tipping is not necessary. And, even if the waiter bows to you, you should not bow back. Save that for your hosts.

You might also acquaint yourself with Japanese culture. Attend a Kabuki or Noh presentation, if there is one around. Or get a video of Kurosawa's *Seven Samurai.* Since you are a businessman, you may be tempted to read more books on doing business in Japan. That should not hurt, at least not too much. It all depends on how informative or misleading they are, with the latter outnumbering the former by at least two or three to one. That is why I am suggesting some good ones now and in the footnotes.

Admittedly, there are other things you could do as well. I have rarely seen them referred to in the basic primers, so I can only assume that they are less important. Still, for completeness sake, let me mention them.

For example, you might contact the nearest office of the Japan External Trade Organization. JETRO, as it is known, has nearly eighty overseas offices in some sixty countries. They are amply staffed with experienced officials who know the Japanese market and can help you develop a feel for it. It offers a broad range of publications, including more general ones on how to find Japanese counterparts, use the distribution system, establish joint ventures and so on. The *Japan Trade Directory* lists most of the companies you could ever want to contact. The *JETRO Marketing Series* covers the basics and *Your Market In Japan* has individual reports on a multitude of product lines. Further useful literature is available in the library.[6]

JETRO will not find you a partner, but it will suggest where to look for one and may mention which trading companies are strongest in specific lines, if that is the route you want to take. By the way, most general trading companies also have offices around the world. So do most major manufacturers, some large retailers, and several prefectures looking for foreign investment.

Over in Japan, you may wish to visit JETRO again. It has a huge office in Tokyo, with abundant staff and an enormous library, and smaller offices in nearly thirty cities. Another helpful body is the Manufactured Imports Promotion Organization (MIPRO) which helps out for sales of manufactures with advice, information, working space and exhibition halls.[7] More recently, the various prefectures have set up "local internationalization centers" which advise on market entry and supply temporary office space.

By now, most foreign embassies in Tokyo can also provide considerable information and some backup through the commercial section. Some countries also assist nationals back home through the Ministry of Trade, Department of Commerce, or special trade offices similar to JETRO like HKTDC or KOTRA in Hong Kong and Korea. The United States Department of Commerce has been making a special effort. It has several programs to help American companies find agents, distributors or clients. It organizes missions and trade shows. Of particular interest is its Japan Export Information Center (JEIC), which offers information and advice on entry strategies, standards and testing, restrictions and barriers, and market research.[8]

While not as entertaining as movies or pop culture, there are some very dull books you might consider which can help you find partners and, equally important, know who your major competitors are. Most useful are the detailed reports by Dodwell Marketing Consultants. One describes the major wholesalers and retailers while others focus on specific industries like electronics, automobiles, etc.[9] Yano Research Institute annually publishes *Market Share in Japan,* indicating the top players in most sectors. You can find more about the listed companies by referring to Toyo Keizai's *Japan Company Handbook.*

What you should be doing, when you are not busy eating *sushi* or practicing bowing, is scrutinizing these and other publications. Before setting foot in Japan, you should know something about the market for your product, who else sells the same line, how the various rivals stack up, who their major shareholders are and what their turnover and profits look like. That may not be culture in the ordinary sense, but it is the best way of making your visit a success.

One last tip. You might reflect on *how* to go. It is not wise just to fly off to Japan without any appointments or introductions. You cannot simply cold call or knock on doors.

Your hosts must be forewarned. That can be done, not terribly well but better than nothing, by writing to those you have singled out. The commercial section of your embassy may be able to help. So can some of the foreign chambers of commerce in Japan. I would strongly recommend contacting the embassy and the chamber well in advance to see what they can do to prepare your trip.

A very interesting alternative is to join a trade mission organized by the U.S. Department of Commerce, Hong Kong Trade Development Council, or whatever national entity is in charge of such things. It will take care of most of the petty and bothersome logistics, like travel, hotels, secretarial and interpreting services, etc. It will also try to attract as many potential Japanese customers or partners as possible. You can then make contacts and perhaps conclude some deals, although that usually takes longer. If you are wise, you can use this as a springboard for a longer stay.

Another springboard is the trade shows or exhibitions, of which there are hundreds, each concentrating on a specific sector. Attend one that covers your line. It is the easiest way of getting broad exposure, meeting potential customers and partners, and also seeing what the competition is offering. Again, the event's organizer may be helpful with accomodations, services, etc. You could extend your stay to follow up on useful contacts.

With this kind of preparation and this kind of introduction, your progress should be much faster and more fruitful than otherwise. To get more details, contact the appropriate national or state office, the relevant trade association or JETRO, the embassy and chamber of commerce. They are there to help you. And don't forget to take along a bunch of gifts to thank everyone who has been helpful. As we all know, the Japanese are great gift givers (and receivers).

NOTES

1. Jackson, N. Huddleston, Jr., *Gaijin Kaisha,* p. 3.
2. On demographic trends and evolving consumer tastes, see George Fields, *Gucci on the Ginza.*
3. *Business America,* September 24, 1990.
4. On the proliferation of small foreign companies, see Helene Thian, *Setting Up & Operating A Business in Japan.*
5. On trade barriers and nontariff barriers, see Michael Czinkota and Jon Woronoff, *Unlocking Japan's Markets,* Clyde V. Prestowitz, Jr., *Trading Places,* and Woronoff, *World Trade War.*
6. More details on JETRO literature are provided in the bibliography. Several addresses are indicated in the Directory.
7. MIPRO's address is in the Directory.
8. JEIC's address is in the Directory.
9. For a complete listing of Dowell publications and further details on the other books, see the Bibliography. Dodwell's address is in the Directory.

2

Corporate Community

Of course, you are going to *Japan* to do business. But Japan is a big place and, no matter how big you are, you will really only be doing business in some small corner of that vast market. So, the sooner the better, you must begin disaggregating and figuring out just what sort of business community you will fit into. Like anywhere else, you must know the players and how they operate. Only then can you decide how best to react.

Unfortunately, most foreign businessmen arrive in Japan and assume either that it is just like back home, with some minor variations, or that it is completely different. Neither extreme is right. But the structure you encounter is more likely to be different than the same. And you will avoid many painful mistakes if you realize that from the outset. The only country in the world with a similar structure is South Korea. Germany comes closest among the Western economies, but even it is considerably more loose and liberal. Comparisons with a free-wheeling place like the United States will probably be wrong.

There are various reasons for this. One, which will be dealt with next, is that companies are organized differently and have some different goals and functions. The very employment system differs. Companies are also much more closely linked, often forming groups not only of allies and associates but potential competitors. If you don't know how they operate and how they cooperate, you are in for many surprises. The following is an effort to clarify the situation enough for you to work out your own position in Japan's corporate community. With luck, it will make your foreign firm a bit less alien.

Companies Large and Small

Foreigners who have never visited Japan, and many who have spent some time there, tend to assume that it is the realm of huge corporations, corporations with immense human and financial resources, offices around the world, and incredible commercial clout. That is not surprising. After all, that is the only kind of company most *gaijin* are exposed to. No matter where we live, we are already familiar with such giants as Mitsui and Mitsubishi, Toyota and Nissan, Bank of Tokyo and Industrial Bank of Japan, Nomura and Daiwa, Matsushita and Hitachi, and many more.

A closer look shows something quite different. These big companies (*dai kigyo*), the ones we know so well, only account for about 1% of all Japanese companies. Admittedly, they employ about 30% of all workers and control a larger amount of assets, sales and so on. But, even considering their size, they remain a minority. The rest are classified as small and medium enterprises (*chu-sho kigyo*) which together amount to 99% of all companies with 70% of the labor force. This juxtaposition of big and small generates what is frequently called a "dual structure."

To some extent, the big companies and smaller ones are in different sectors. The overwhelming majority of the smaller enterprises are in construction, distribution (mom-and-pop stores) or services (fast food, personal and business services, leisure). But many are in manufacturing, frequently in more backward areas but sometimes in quite advanced ones. Often the big and small share a sector, the big banks and the small consumer loan firms, the big automakers and the small parts suppliers, the big steel mills and the small fabricators. To understand Japan, it is indispensable to consider both.

To function in Japan, it is necessary to deal with both and remember that they often operate on a different basis. For example, big companies recruit the best students from the best schools; small ones get what is left over. Big companies offer "lifetime employment," at least to the extent it exists. Small companies tend to hire and fire more readily. Employees of big companies earn more, work less and enjoy better conditions than employees of small companies. We shall see what this means to the Japanese and to foreigners doing business in Japan further on.

A more decisive aspect of the duality is that smaller companies are often dependent on or at least beholden to larger companies. In distribution, small stores and shops frequently sell the produce of the large companies. Small service firms curry to their needs. Small factories busily turn out parts and components that big companies assemble into finished products. But they rarely do so as free agents. There is one link or another which establishes a fairly rigid, hierarchical relationship. That is the key to so much of what happens in Japan that a foreigner will never know his way around without studying these relationships.

Groups and Keiretsu

In Japan, it is not enough to know the players as such, it is essential to know with which other companies they have close relations of one sort or another. Only then can you evaluate their true strength and potential and decide whether to work with or avoid them. That is because links are so prevalent and so important. Virtually every company is tied to many others in various ways which reinforce or restrict its action. Frequently, these links are highly structured and form a clearly definable circle of associates or a full-fledged group.[1]

There are three basic types of links or "alignments" you should watch for since they fashion the three basic types of groups or *keiretsu*. One is a circle of large companies which revolves around a bank and is thus called a bank or capital group. The second is a coterie of smaller suppliers and sub-contractors organized by a large manufacturer which is known as an enterprise group. The third consists of captive outlets of major producers, the distribution group.

Most familiar is the bank group or *kin'yu keiretsu* which in some cases grew out of the earlier *zaibatsu* and in others resulted from efforts of rising banks to emulate them. This alignment brings together major players in just about every important sector, not only a bank but a trading company, insurers, assorted manufacturers and some service establishments. These companies are relatively independent and equal members which cooperate in their mutual interest, either to do business with one another or launch joint projects. You will recognize the names of leading ones like Mitsui, Mitsubishi, Sumitomo, Fuyo (Fuji), Dai-Ichi Kangyo, Sanwa, etc. (See page 31.)

The enterprise group (*kigyo keiretsu*) is basically a network of suppliers and subcontractors for manufacturers and thus looks rather familiar. But it is a much tighter unit than elsewhere, since the suppliers are much more dependent on the manufacturer, to the extent where their operations are partly integrated in its own. There is also a greater tendency to buy only within this network and not go outside even if cheaper supplies could be obtained. Such groups can be found in many sectors, autos, ships, steel, chemicals, electronics. Familiar names are Toyota and Nissan, Nippon Steel, Asahi Chemical, Hitachi, Toshiba, Sony and so on. (See page 39.)

The distribution groups (*ryutsu keiretsu*) involve distributors for many consumer goods, from automobiles to household appliances, from watches to eyeglasses, including also cosmetics and electronics. The wholesalers and retailers are

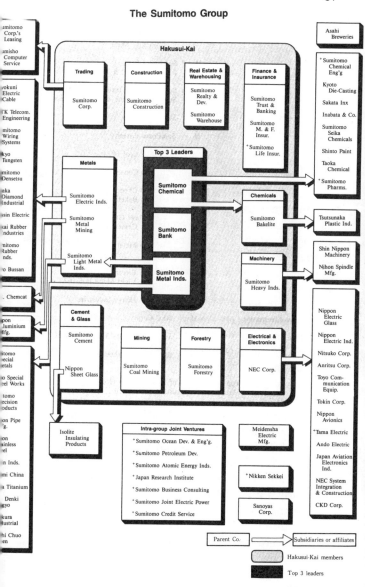

31

Source: Dodwell Marketing Consultants, *Industrial Groupings In Japan*, 1991, p. 78.

again more dependent than elsewhere. They are also particularly numerous, running into the thousands and even tens of thousands. More decisive, captive outlets may account for the majority of all outlets with even supposedly "independent" ones restricted to several Japanese makes. There is no need to name names, any producer in the sector must have its own network if it is to prosper.

While the three categories can be distinguished conceptually, it is worthwhile noting that many leading companies belong to more than one. Manufacturers are often part of a bank *keiretsu,* they have their own subcontracting network and sell through a circle of related distributors. The best examples are the automakers and electronics firms. This makes the "big" Japanese companies much bigger than they appear at first sight. For what it is worth, it also makes the "small" enterprises weaker and more dependent.

There is a tendency to tell gullible foreigners that these groups are just the result of Japanese preferences for stable, long-term relations. That sounds good, reasonable and irreprochable. But the realities are quite different. Links are based not on affinity but material control through share crossholding in bank groups and financial domination of suppliers and retailers through shareholding, loans and advances. Large companies also appoint key personnel in smaller ones or impose on them by being the sole supplier or buyer.

Why this interest in *keiretsu?* Because they are major pillars of the Japanese business community? Because you will encounter them everywhere you turn? Because you must adjust to them? Yes. That. And one thing more. The *keiretsu* are an immense market in themselves. The eight largest account for nearly a fifth of Japan's turnover. They also do a lot of business amongst themselves, about 13% of intergroup transactions for the looser bank groups and as much as 30–50% for the enterprise groups.[2] This means that, if you can tie up with a *keiretsu,* you may have privileged access to major clients. On the other hand, you may have trouble dealing with companies in other groups.

Business Organizations

The Japanese are also big believers in business organizations. Most of them appear rather familiar. You have something like that, or at least called by the same name, in your own country. But they often possess greater prerogatives and prestige in Japan. You should seriously consider whether to join, not for social but business reasons. You may not. You may wish to stay aloof. But you can be certain that they are still aware of your presence.

Particularly interesting are the trade associations.[3] They exist for just about every conceivable sector. Some sprang up spontaneously, others were instigated by the government because the establishment feels that the existence of such organizations makes for a stabler, stronger economy. Sometimes the sectors are quite narrow so that larger foreign companies may fall under the purview of several.

These trade associations bring together all the major players and some of the minor ones but not every last firm. Together with officials in the relevant ministry, they work out regulations that should apply to their activities. Companies also cooperate to define technical standards. While not strictly legitimate, they tend to be somewhat restrictive in that they do not readily accept newcomers and foreigners, alas, are often newcomers. *Gaishi* are also harder to assimilate. To join, and there are definite advantages, foreign companies must show they can conform to the rules and are sometimes supervised until they become fully accepted.

Even when not overly hospitable, contacts with the trade association can be extremely useful. For one, it is possible to learn which companies do what and which might eventually become partners or associates. One can get a better idea of how the sector is regulated and policed. The trade association is keenly aware of what the government is planning and it usually plays a crucial role in shaping new legislation and regulations.

The Japan Chamber of Commerce and Industry, and the local chambers, are not only more familiar, they tend to function more like their counterparts abroad. Given the clannishness of Japanese companies and the difficulty in meeting their executives more informally, this can be an excellent entree. It is also much easier for *gaijin* to join. But do not expect to achieve too much concretely.

The real source of power in the business community is the Japan Federation of Economic Organizations or Keidanren, which brings together the largest companies in an extremely influential forum. Similar bodies abroad are a mere shadow of it. Keidanren not only advises the political leaders, it funds them. It not only discusses problems with senior bureaucrats, it usually imposes its line on them. But you will have to follow its activities from afar. It is not likely to welcome foreign members.

Where the *gaishi* can go, and most definitely should go, is the foreign chamber if one exists for your country. There is an American, British, Dutch, French, German and Italian chamber as well as one for the European Community.[4] There are looser organizations for some other nationalities. These bodies are a source of information, a place to meet counterparts and learn from more experienced Japan hands, and a good starting point in seeking partners and associates or consultants and lawyers. The chambers also try to influence the Japanese government with regard to foreign interests.

Japan is no place for loners, whether individuals or companies. More than elsewhere, it is necessary to belong. And what you belong to can make a very big difference in your future success.

Government Relations

Many foreign businessmen, especially Western ones, do not think much of the government's role. They come from countries where it is relatively minor and companies are free to conduct their affairs as they like, within the limits of the law. There is not much to be gained from currying favor with government leaders or even listening to what they have to say. They would be foolish to assume that they can go about their business as freely in Japan.

In Japan, government does matter. It matters very much. It does considerably more than just lay down a broad framework in which business can be conducted. It often works out rather minute procedures which must be followed. These procedures, by the way, may not even be written or exist in a sense. They are provided not only by laws, regulations and the like but "administrative guidance" (*gyosei shido*). This is advice, formulated case-by-case for specific circumstances and which may well not be repeated even in similar circumstances. The only way to obtain it is to ask specifically and violating such unwritten rules, even if they are not known, would be most impolitic.[5]

Admittedly, when I speak of the government's role, I am not thinking of the role of the politicians. They may be uppermost in Western and developing societies; in Japan, it is the bureaucrats who call the shots. It is therefore necessary to get to know the bureaucrats in your sector. This means officials of the Finance Ministry for banks, insurance and securities firms, Ministry of International Trade and Industry for manufacturers, Ministry of Health for pharmaceuticals, etc.

These officials can inform you about the various intricate regulations existing for imports. They can give you pointers on how to—and not to—conduct business in your line. They grant all sorts of permits and authorizations . . . or not, depending on what they think of you. Of course, you will not be able to deal with senior officials at the outset. You will have to make do with quite junior personnel who should be treated with great respect not because of their ability but their position and what they can do to help or hinder your efforts. Anyway, with time, they will rise and become more influential.

While most rules and regulations are neutral and apply equally to everyone, you are bound to encounter some which appear biased against your company or foreigners in general. There used to be thousands of them. Now there may just be hundreds. For the ministries have been severely criticized by foreign governments and endeavor to appear more enlightened. Be that as it may, you may well run into a remaining nontariff barrier or superfluous regulation whose compliance demands costly and time-consuming efforts.

If a regulation works against you, something must be done other than allowing it to stymie your progress. That something can be a complaint to your embassy, which may or may not wish to help out. If it does, it may influence the bureaucracy in your favor. It may also get their backs up. So the first effort should probably be a gentle, diplomatic one with a resort to official recourse only later. By the way, the Japanese government has appointed an ombudsman to look into grievances. Unfortunately, so far he has been neither quick nor effective.

Where Do You Fit In?

The above information was not provided to expand your cultural outlook or emphasize just how different those Japanese are. The purpose was to describe the lay of the land so that when you move in you have a better idea of what to expect. The new guy on the block should always be aware of who is around and who really counts. He should know his neighborhood and try to fit in. Fitting in is particularly important in Japan because the Japanese expect newcomers to adapt as smoothly as possible and without creating too much fuss and bother for the old-timers.

For one, you might remember that size matters in Japan. How big you are counts almost as much as who you are in a dual structure where the big and small behave quite differently and interrelate in specific ways. You should realize that your own behavior should differ if you are a large, prestigious foreign firm or a tiny, inconsequential one. Forget any notions of all being equal or making up for size with imagination and drive. That is not the prevailing ethos and— on the surface at least—knowing your place is useful.

By the way, in this polarized arena of very large and very small, you may discover that you are not as small as you thought. You may still be considerably larger than your counterparts in certain sectors or certain activities where small firms are prevalent, such as services and distribution. On the other hand, even if you are quite big back home, once you consider the group relationships of your potential partners or competitors, you may discover that they are bigger than you thought.

Big and small is just the start. There is a definite tendency for the former to dominate the latter. Relations are much more structured and equality is not even a theoretical goal. In particular, suppliers and subcontractors should expect stiffer conditions than back home. They will also have less leverage and less chance to work with a broad array of customers. If you cannot accept such relations, if you cannot comply with such conditions, there is not much point to looking for business in Japan.

On the other hand, if you happen to be buying goods from Japanese suppliers, you can expect them to go that extra mile. They will go out of their way to satisfy whatever conditions you may lay down. They will find it quite normal that the conditions are strict. Indeed, if you are too lax or lenient, they are quite likely to loose respect for your company. You should know where you fit in not only when you are below but when you are on top.

In a business community in which local companies have multiple relations with other companies, especially associates, it is hard to go it alone. This may be your philosophy back home. It would be wise to modify it in Japan. Even if you can produce your own parts, sell your own goods, finance your own needs, it is extremely useful just to make friends who can do the same thing for you. In some cases, they cannot do it any better; in others, they can. However, the simple fact of doing business with you will increase their interest in your succeeding and they may help out in ways you would not expect.

In Japan, competition is fierce. It is often nastier than abroad. Yet, even competitors know how to cooperate in their mutual interest. This can be done through the trade associations or more informal gatherings. It can be done by adjusting relations with other sectors or the government. But so much is going on that a mere bystander will miss it. Participating is more purposeful. It will not make you an insider, certainly not quickly. But it will at least make your *gaishi* less of an outsider in a society that does not really like outsiders.

Given the prevalence of groups, and the tight and chummy relations between group members, it would be smart always to check on who associates with whom. This should apply to your competitors, since you want to know just how strong they are. You want to know who their bankers are, who their suppliers are, who distributes their goods and so on. You also want to know how strong any links are and what they imply for you. That much is obvious.

Less obvious is that you must scrutinize potential partners more than elsewhere. You must find out who their associates are, their bankers, suppliers, distributors, etc. That way you

The Toshiba Group

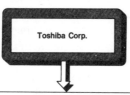

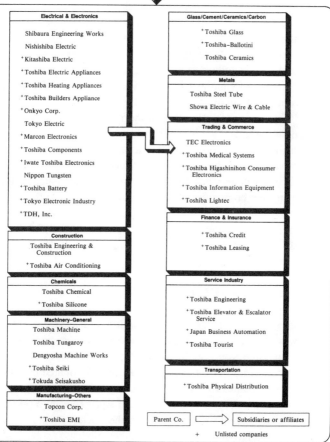

Electrical & Electronics

Shibaura Engineering Works

Nishishiba Electric

+ Kitashiba Electric

+ Toshiba Electric Appliances

+ Toshiba Heating Appliances

+ Toshiba Builders Appliance

+ Onkyo Corp.

Tokyo Electric

+ Marcon Electronics

+ Toshiba Components

+ Iwate Toshiba Electronics

Nippon Tungsten

+ Toshiba Battery

+ Tokyo Electronic Industry

+ TDH, Inc.

Construction

Toshiba Engineering & Construction

+ Toshiba Air Conditioning

Chemicals

Toshiba Chemical

+ Toshiba Silicone

Machinery-General

Toshiba Machine

Toshiba Tungaroy

Dengyosha Machine Works

+ Toshiba Seiki

+ Tokuda Seisakusho

Manufacturing-Others

Topcon Corp.

+ Toshiba EMI

Glass/Cement/Ceramics/Carbon

+ Toshiba Glass

+ Toshiba-Ballotini

Toshiba Ceramics

Metals

Toshiba Steel Tube

Showa Electric Wire & Cable

Trading & Commerce

TEC Electronics

+ Toshiba Medical Systems

+ Toshiba Higashinihon Consumer Electronics

+ Toshiba Information Equipment

+ Toshiba Lightec

Finance & Insurance

+ Toshiba Credit

+ Toshiba Leasing

Service Industry

+ Toshiba Engineering

+ Toshiba Elevator & Escalator Service

+ Japan Business Automation

+ Toshiba Tourist

Transportation

+ Toshiba Physical Distribution

| Parent Co. | ⟹ | Subsidiaries or affiliates |

+ Unlisted companies

it: Dodwell Marketing Consultants, *Industrial Groupings In Japan,* 1991, p. 217.

will know just how strong they are, how much they can contribute to any joint effort. You can also discover just how eager they are to contribute. After all, it is possible that even if the prospective partner is not a direct competitor, it may have associates within the broader *keiretsu* who are. And this could crimp its style.

If you can adopt this approach in dealing with Japanese companies, your chances of success will be immeasurably greater. For that is how they operate. They do not think solely of their own interests or the relationship with your company but how this all affects the broader business community. That was clearly stated by Mark Zimmerman, former president of the American Chamber of Commerce in Japan and head of several joint ventures.

"The questions revolving in the mind of a Japanese contemplating a deal are how the industrial group with which he is affiliated will view the new arrangement with a foreign company; what the association of his industry will have to say; and whether he will be taking unfair advantage, thus causing his competitors to react violently. In fact, the Japanese is as concerned with the impact of the agreement on his standing within the Japanese business community as he is with direct monetary benefits that his firm will derive from the arrangements."[6]

More Homework Before You Go

I hate to be so demanding, but before you leave for Japan, it would be exceedingly useful to do some more homework.

This time you should do very careful research on your sector in order to determine whether it is dominated by a few large companies or spread among many small ones, so you know whether you stand a chance of squeezing in. You may get some insight into that through the documentation of the trade association or at least the membership list. *Market Share in Japan* will let you know which ones are on top. Further information can be obtained from JETRO, the embassy or local business consultants.

Even more important, you should check on your potential partners and competitors. This time it is not a question of what their products are, what they cost, how they compare. It is more a matter of determining who they are related to for the reasons just mentioned. You do not want to find out that your competitors are stronger than you thought, that your prospective partner is weaker or that is is hampered by relations with other companies.

It is not easy to trace all the links. But the Dodwell publications certainly point you in the right direction. *Industrial Groupings in Japan* indicates the membership of the largest groups with lists not only of the members but many of their own subsidiaries and affiliates. Insight into enterprise groups is provided in the volumes on the electronics and automobile industries. You will have a fairly good idea of what is supplied within the "family," what possible gaps may exist and who you will have to compete with if you want the business.

Naturally, such literature only covers the major sectors and companies. It also only has so much information. To fill in the gaps, it may be necessary to have more exhaustive studies run by appropriate bodies. Your embassy or foreign chamber of commerce can probably provide names of reliable companies specialized in this sort of research.

*   *   *

This is the last time I will suggest specific homework since you should have more than enough to keep you busy once you arrive in Japan. However, I would recommend further reading. Obviously, each of these chapters is much too small to go into detail on all aspects and some excellent books (as well as some pretty mediocre ones) are available to fill in

with additional information. I would strongly urge you to
read some of them and therefore list more useful books or
publications in the footnotes. They are presented in full, with
publisher, in the bibliography.

NOTES

1. For an analysis of the different types of groupings and their impact on
   business, see Czinkota and Woronoff, op. cit., pp. 31–74. For membership of the leading groups, see Dodwell, *Industrial Groupings in
   Japan*. For further details on enterprise groups in the electronics and auto
   parts sectors, see Dodwell, *Key Players in the Japanese Electronics
   Industry* and *The Structure of the Japanese Auto Parts Industry*.
2. Marie Anchordoguy, ''A Brief History of Japan's Keiretsu,'' *Harvard
   Business Review*, July–August 1990, p. 59.
3. On the role of trade associations, see Leonard H. Lynn and Timothy J.
   McKeown, *Organizing Business*.
4. For addresses of some foreign chambers, see the Directory.
5. On the government's role in the economy, see Woronoff, *Japanese
   Targeting*.
6. Mark Zimmerman, *How To Do Business With The Japanese*, pp.
   100–1.

3

Business-Related Culture

Somewhere along the line, most books on doing business in Japan lapse into fanciful reflections on Japanese culture. They muse about the ancient customs and traditions, how the Japanese personality is forged by mutual obligation (*giri* and *on*) or the time-honored loyalty of the *samurai* toward his lord. They explain how flower arrangement or tea ceremony or goodness knows what shapes the inner workings of the Japanese mind. Foreigners must be very sensitive and subtle in adjusting to these cultural factors if they are to succeed in the business world, it is argued.

No! Well, yes and no. There is not the slightest doubt that culture has a deep and pervasive influence on the Japanese, like everybody else, and that cultural factors must be considered. But they tend to pick the wrong factors and impute rather exotic and far-fetched consequences. Most of today's Japanese, the living, breathing ones you are likely to meet, are affected by very different conditions and impulses. They are much more real and much more effective. And, if you miss them, you could do quite poorly in trying both to comprehend Japan and make some money there.

After all, aside from the older business and government leaders (many already in semi-retirement), most company executives, ministry officials, workers and consumers are heirs to a very different culture. One that is more open, one that is more affluent and one that has forgotten so many of the ancient and honorable ways that their parents and grand-parents wonder just how Japanese they are. In fact, when Japanese companies send their employees off to a foreign posting nowadays, they have to first be taught what ''Japanese culture'' is all about so as to answer questions from inquisitive foreigners.

Lifetime Employment

One of the practical manifestations you are bound to en-counter is what is loosely called ''lifetime employment.'' This embodies not only a different form of recruitment, pro-motion, remuneration and so on, it creates a different work world. It is extremely important to understand what the im-plications are for the Japanese—and also the foreign busi-nessmen—if ever you are to establish your own company here or even use the services of a local one. But forget about quaint notions of the company family, the caring employer, the loyal worker and the like. The explanations are cruder and more forceful.

As a start, of course, you should realize that lifetime em-ployment does not exist in all companies. It takes a rather large one to recruit enough personnel to make the system meaningful. It therefore prevails in the upper tier (actually perhaps 10%) of the companies by number with perhaps 40% of the total work force. The rest, smaller and even medium-sized firms, just emulate it in some ways or merely pay lip service. Even where it exists, it most emphatically does not include women, part-time or temporary workers or those who joined the company part way through their career. So, at best 15–20% of the total labor force is included.

A further point. It is not ''lifetime.'' The system covers employees from entry until the official retirement age, which varies from company to company but it now about 57. Most still have to work until the age of 60, 65 and more to get by.

Other employees are dropped even before reaching retirement. We are told that dismissal *only* occurs in exceptional circumstances and for grievous misbehavior. Maybe so. Alas, companies also shed staff by transferring them to suppliers and subcontractors, by setting up small firms to absorb them or just suggesting that they would be wise to retire now with a bonus rather than hang around.

How does the system work . . . for those lucky enough to enjoy it? That can not be entirely summarized in the following, and much more background can be found in *Japan's Wasted Workers* and other books listed in the bibliography.[1] Still, some salient features convey the essence.

First of all, youngsters are recruited directly from school, whether a high school, vocational school or college. They have no previous experience and, in case you are interested, their employers like it that way. They want to form young, impressionable workers in their own manner and turn them into loyal employees. That explains why so much emphasis is placed on education, or rather, graduating from the right schools since major companies tend to recruit from the same sources. This is done year after year and each year a large, relatively undifferentiated crop of young school leavers is harvested.

These new employees are distributed among the various offices and plants and trained on the job. There may be some formal training, but not all that much. The rest comes from watching what older workers do and being integrated in the team. Most will stay in a given posting for two or three years and then rotate to another, regularly at this rhythm, getting to know the company and its personnel extremely well. Those on the fast track will *not* specialize. They remain generalists. Specialists, engineers, mechanics, designers, bookkeepers and the like will be stuck in the same place much longer and rarely reach the top.

As employees are rotated, they also rise gradually. They

move up with the "career escalator," from year to year, with a steadily rising salary and increasingly more impressive title. What they do in each assignment, how capable they are, how dedicated they are, how long working and long suffering they are will make relatively little difference during most of the ride. Seniority is the rule. The big difference comes when the few are selected to become executives and the many are sent off to subsidiaries or suppliers or asked to retire gracefully.

However, before thinking how nice it is . . . at least for those who reach the top, let me interject that there is not just one escalator. There are several. One is for male college graduates, which starts part way up and goes from modest white-collar positions to company president sometimes. There is another for male high school graduates, which allocates blue-collar jobs that may eventually lead to a supervisory post in the factory. The third and fourth are for women, with high school graduates sent to the assembly lines and college graduates entering the offices, but with less responsibility and chance of promotion. For them, "lifetime" employment is rather short, just a few years until they get married, have children or become a bore.

Worse, many female employees are very poorly used even while they are around. This applies much less to the factory workers than the white or pink-collar employees. They are given rather little incentive to perform well and even less initiative. Indeed, many are relegated to humdrum tasks like running errands, taking phone calls and typing letters. That is, when they are not busy ushering in customers or serving tea. They are given the informal title of "office lady" or OL. But it is a frightful waste of time and talent.

When you do business with the Japanese, you will meet almost exclusively "lifetime employees," from the president down to the girl serving tea. These are company men (or women) who are probably more devoted to their company's success than you are to that of your own. Don't forget that. It is not a question of cooperation, or harmonious relations or give-and-take, they were sent to win and the personal commitment and urge to win is much greater. On the other hand, if doing business with you will enhance their chances of winning (especially against other Japanese companies), they can be very sturdy—if not entirely trustworthy—allies.

That is just one of the consequences of this modern Japanese business culture. There are many others, some of which will be discussed in the following sections. So, put aside your copy of *The Chrysanthemum and the Sword* or *The Book of Five Rings* and consider some realities.

Company Loyalty

Enthusiastic commentators compare today's "salaryman," the ubiquitous, all-purpose white-collar employee with yesteryear's *samurai*. Certainly, the *sarariman* is devoted to his company, dependent on his company and willing to sacrifice his time and even personal life for his company. He will stay with his company through thick and thin until the "lifetime" stint is over. But that has less to do with *giri* and obligation than other, more compelling factors.

Company employees are loyal because of the lifetime employment system. First of all, they are recruited directly from school and have no previous experience of another company, so they can hardly compare employers. In addition, few are specialized enough to offer specific skills to any other employer. All they know, and that they know exceedingly well, is how their own company operates and who does what. But that is hardly transferable. Nobody else would hire them just for that.

Given the cult of loyalty throughout corporate Japan, few other large companies would want to hire them if they left their earlier employer even if they did have special skills.

True, there has been some job hopping of late. But most companies do not like "traitors" or find it easy to integrate anyone who joins them in mid-career or, indeed, anywhere but the bottom of the escalator. Added to this, of course, there is an unwritten no-poaching rule among many companies. We will not lure your people, you will not take ours.

It is the escalator itself which increases the hang for loyalty. Each year, as it ascends, you earn a bit more and rise through the ranks with seniority. By the time you have been with the company ten years, you have a reasonable wage, an enhanced status and a fairly comfortable position. It would be unwise to risk that under any circumstances. But it would be particularly silly to do so by moving to another Japanese company. For then, you would probably have to start at or near the bottom and in a staff that does not like to absorb newcomers. That is quite different from the Western situation, where most change jobs in the expectation of yet more money, prestige and acceptance.

The lifetime employment system not only keeps most Japanese in their place, it enhances the desirability of entering large companies which can more readily provide lifetime employment. It adds to the attraction of growing companies, because they will find it easier to offer promotions and carry staff longer. Above all, it favors Japanese companies which are assumed to keep their employees come what may as opposed to Western or Asian companies which just hire and fire without regard to the employee's fate.

This presentation may not be as inspiring as the tale of the forty-seven *ronin* who followed their master even into death. But it does more to explain what foreign companies are likely to face when they seek Japanese personnel. For one, it will be much harder to recruit than in places where there is greater mobility. For another, most available candidates will be either rather young or rather old. And there may be some doubt about the future loyalty of any who happen to be available in mid-career.

While loyalty is real, but for different reasons than assumed, harmony (*wa*) seems to be more of a fiction. Certainly, there is harmony against everything outside the company. Within, however, it is quite another matter. Employees are jockeying for position so that they can take the escalator to the top and not be shoved off along the way. To do so, they frequently form factions whose struggle for power is as ruthless as anywhere in the world, though better concealed from public view. The stakes are high, namely the control of the only company they can work for.

You may assume this does not affect you. You are perhaps wrong. There may be one faction that likes working with your company and enjoys foreign exposure while another is more insular or just doesn't care for this particular relationship. Which faction comes out on top can be crucial for you as well, although I would not suggest mixing in company politics to affect the outcome. Still, if your guys lose, you had better start thinking of alternative arrangements.

It is obvious to anyone familiar with Japan that harmony is preached more fervently than it is practiced. Yet, you will hear ceaseless references to *wa*. They will come either from naive Westerners or devious Japanese.[2] The latter will suggest that you, the foreigner, should make every effort to get into line with Japanese mores, usually in a way that benefits them more than you. You may hear similar appeals for trust, human relations and so on. So, do pay lip service, but don't let them take advantage of you. This is all part of the *tatemae* (illusion) and not the *honne* (reality) of Japanese being.

All Is Not Well

This employment system, which defines the corporate culture in which most Japanese employees live, generates not only positive characteristics, like dedication, loyalty, hard work and so on. There are negative features as well. These failings are hardly ever referred to by the Japanese, since they either deny or hide them. Even most foreign observers have not noticed their existence. But they can be extremely important for foreign businessmen. Without wishing to overdo the parallel, it is the astute warrior who exploits his opponent's weaknesses. And it is necessary to seek them out.

One which may come as a surprise to most *gaijin,* who have never heard anything bad about Japanese workers, is that they are not as competent as might be desired. It is not just that I have personally met a large number of inefficient, sloppy or ignorant ones. They exist in abundance, just like everywhere else. What is more serious is that the system generates whole classes of incompetents.

You have doubtlessly heard of the Peter Principle according to which employees rise to the level of their incompetence. They are good at what they do, and get promoted to a position where they are also good, and then get promoted again. Somewhere along the line they get promoted too far and are incapable of handling the job. Now, this happens in an employment system where people are promoted on the basis (largely) of ability. Can you imagine what must happen when people are promoted on the basis (largely) of seniority?

The First Woronoff Principle is that Japanese are frequently unable to fulfill their responsibilities. They get promoted regularly, with the years, and a year older is not necessarily a year wiser. Worse, they get promoted into positions not on the basis of personal ability but the fact that the seat is empty because the former inhabitant was promoted further up. Not because they have been groomed for it, not because they have taken special training, not because they show a natural aptitude or anything else.

The Second Woronoff Principle, if this is not presumptuous, is that rotation generates large numbers of incompetents at all levels and all times. Clearly, when you are transferred to a new office, with new responsibilities and new colleagues, you cannot possibly know what to do. It takes time to learn. Most Japanese reckon about a year. They also feel that toward the third year, since you know you will soon be transferred out, employees tend to become slack and unconcerned. After all, come the next rotation and they will have left. That is pretty bad when you consider that employees may not be in their best form two years out of three.

On to the Third Woronoff Principle. Rotation has further drawbacks. I would be the first to admit that it forms employees with a profound knowledge of how the company operates. I already said that. But it is extremely difficult to develop professional knowhow when you are regularly shunted about, from personnel to sales, from sales to manufacturing, off to an overseas branch and back to a remote local subsidiary, and so on. And this in no logical order. It is thus impossible to develop any expertise or professionalism and even the Japanese concede this weakness.

Why then don't outsiders notice these weaknesses? To be perfectly frank, it is usually because foreigners are so starry-eyed and have been stuffed with such nonsense about Japanese efficiency by gullible academics that they cannot imagine that flaws exist, let alone look for them. But it can contribute greatly to your own effectiveness if you do realize that incompetence is alive and well in Japan, and not only the United States, France, the Philippines or wherever you come from.

For one, if things are actually being accomplished, then it may not be the person holding the formal title who is doing this but an assistant. There may be a junior employee who, either for love of the company, or affection for his superior, or because someone has to pitch in, actually assumes the responsibilities. He will earn Brownie points and perhaps rise to the top. That is a person you should cultivate.

Another pointer, when negotiating with the Japanese, do

not assume that just because there is a pregnant silence the assembled businessmen are cogitating and coming up with a superlative response. They may just as well be puzzled and not know what to do. If you send a letter and don't get a reply, it may be because they cannot get their act together. If they do something stupid, it does not have to be a trap. It is not those wily Japanese who are trying to trick you. They can make mistakes, too. And you had better take advantage of them as they would benefit from your foolish moves.

On the other hand, don't complain about their blunders or tell them they are foolish. Protocol forbids. And the Japanese are particularly irked to be caught out or made to lose face. If you have the intelligence to realize that they goofed, have the tact not to say so outright.

Inefficiency Amidst Efficiency

If there is so much incompetence, how can Japanese companies succeed as brilliantly as they do? That can best be explained by disaggregating. It is not all companies which succeed but mainly the larger ones, especially those in manufacturing. Their secret has been to devise the most extraordinary system of motivating blue-collar workers and running efficient factories. What they say in the books is true, if somewhat embellished. Manufacturing is handled superbly.

Blue-collar workers are well-trained. They are flexible, moving from job to job as necessary. Their machinery is productive and put to the best use. There is a constant effort to improve yet further, you know, *kaizen*.[3] Move the machinery a bit, change the design a bit, make your employees work a bit smarter, save a yen here and there and you are well ahead. If the work can be done better by machines, automate and bring in the robots. There will be no complaint from the workers who are either happy to get cleaner, safer jobs or are too dependent on the company to resist.

In addition, make the workers contribute to this effort. Obviously, nobody knows their job as well as they do and if anyone can suggest improvements, they can. So you form quality control circles and have them meet regularly to boost quality. You hold productivity campaigns and offer modest monetary rewards but ample prestige and promotions to get more suggestions. The workers cannot gripe if jobs are lost. After all, who made the suggestions?

You will not find much of this even in the administration of the same companies. White-collar workers are not organized as strictly, each man in his post, doing exactly what he should do, and constantly improving on that. They sit around in big, sprawling offices, with papers piled high on the desks and not even file cabinets to keep them in order. There are computers, but they are often off in a corner and operated by the lowly "office lady," since become a "computer lady." The more exalted male employees do not do that. In fact, they haven't discovered the telephone's usefulness yet. When they telephone, it is not to settle a business arrangement but to make an appointment.

White-collar employees spend an inordinate time with two activities. One is to coordinate with colleagues. This involves such quaint practices as *ringi-sho* and *nemawashi,* dear to the hearts of foreign academics. The first is a written proposal by an underling which passes through the corporate hierarchy until everyone has signed on (i.e. put his personal seal on it). *Nemawashi* or "root-binding" involves endless one-on-one negotiations to obtain acceptance from everybody. And this means everybody. No such thing as a majority decision. Admirable . . . if you are an academic. Horrible if you are trying to run a company efficiently.[4]

The other activity is to travel all over town, all over the country and all over the world to discuss business. The Japanese adore face-to-face encounters. They feel most comfortable working out details in person. They also like a chance to get out of the office and perhaps enjoy an interesting trip, hearty meals and cheerful drinking paid for by the company. Settle it by phone? Send a fax? Much too impersonal for the Japanese. But foreigners find it much cheaper, much faster, much more efficient. Another place where we are one up on the Japanese.

Not only are the offices inefficient, so are the distribution networks. As will be seen later, there are more wholesalers and retailers per customer in Japan than other advanced countries. Not only a bit more. About twice as many. This is sheer inefficiency. It adds tremendously to costs and involves more people in shifting products rather than making them. One reason Japan has succeeded is that it could sell many of its efficiently produced manufactures in efficient Western and Asian outlets, combining its strength with ours. Alas, we have to sell *our* goods through *their* distributors, which is not half as nice.

When it comes to inefficiency—as normally measured— there is nothing more inefficient than Japan's services. And the inefficiency increases the closer you get to the end user, especially the ordinary consumer. They demand ''service,'' which sounds fair. Of course, they have a right to prompt delivery, perhaps also nice wrapping paper and pretty boxes, even after-sales service if the thing breaks down. But, and this is less sensible, they tend to favor establishments with superfluous and supercilious personnel. They want people to bow and scrape and treat them as exalted customers, which boosts their egos but not the nation's productivity.

So much for Japanese efficiency. Yes, efficiency in the factory. Efficiency in parts of banking. Efficiency in modern services. But not much to be seen in distribution or more traditional services. And, as I indicated in *Japan's Wasted Workers,* no managers enrolled in QC circles or making useful suggestions. That is for lesser mortals.

Again, how does this affect you, the foreigner? Well, if

the Japanese are as good as claimed at manufacturing, you had better improve your own performance. On the other hand, if you are in distribution, the services or even parts of manufacturing they have neglected, you may well be more efficient than they are. You may know some tricks they do not. You may be able to outclass them.

Hierarchy Above All

There is one last cultural feature which must never be forgotten. This undergirds and overarches all the others. It is hierarchy. This is a silent principle. It is not expressly stated and may actually be downplayed. Much of it has traditional roots, but a lot was concocted by management more recently. While it can be spontaneous, if one does not comply voluntarily compulsion can be used. Whatever the cause, the effect is that everybody in Japan knows his position in the hierarchy and this explains much of what he or she does.

Hierarchy takes many forms. Many, many forms. Perhaps more surprising in a company setting is the role of seniority. I said seniority, not age. What counts is how long a person has been with the company, not how old he is, and a recent transferee will have to bow to younger men who have been with the company longer. Another good reason not to engage in job hopping. Age only counts for things like retirement and birthdays (you are allowed to have those).

Seniority is not an abstract concept. It is worked into the employment system. As noted, employees rise gradually over the years. Later on, some attain high positions. The others tend to leave since it is hard to take orders from a junior. Senior and junior are not just sociological terms, each has to interact with the other in specified ways, using certain words, adopting expected attitudes, bowing in the prescribed manner. There is never any doubt who is the superior so, when managers walk about factories or sit in the common canteen, ordinary workers never have any doubt who they are.

Discrimination by sex also exists. Women, as noted, are much less likely to be promoted or even to stay with the company very long. But that is not all. They, too, are expected to behave, speak and bow appropriately, namely in a way that demeans them and exalts their male colleagues. In most cases, this implies even younger male colleagues although now some women have attained a position that outranks ordinary workers.

Race does not play much of a role since the Japanese are, or at least claim to be, homogeneous. Of course, the Japanese of Korean and Chinese origin are somewhat less homogeneous. The same applies for previous condition of servitude, except for the *burakumin* whose increasingly remote ancestors were in the wrong trades. Now, however, there is an added complication in that foreigners have to be integrated in the hierarchy. They include laborers from Asia and even further afield, skilled and unskilled, Westerners who simply decided to stay and mostly hold white-collar jobs, and executives posted here by foreign companies. This is a rather broad mix of *gaijin* and they will quickly learn that they are not all treated alike.

Beyond this hierarchy of persons there is a hierarchy of companies. Big companies certainly enjoy more prestige than smaller ones that do not work with them. Smaller ones that are subsidiaries, suppliers or subcontractors are in a distinctly inferior position. Suppliers in general, companies engaged in distribution, services and the like are always beholden to the exalted customer, be it an individual or corporate entity. This difference in status not only affects the company per se but any person who represents it, from top to bottom. Finally, those in business are on a lower rung than bureaucrats. It is hard to tell where politicians fit in . . . but it is not very high up.

Nothing could be more mistaken than to assume that, as

a foreign businessman, this may be culturally interesting but of no practical significance. Quite to the contrary. You are also expected to know your rank (or that of your company) and to abide by the proper etiquette. The Japanese will doubtlessly realize that you are not fully aware of the pecking order, cannot judge your exact position and may not know the fine points of formal conduct. They will expect some uncertainty and awkwardness. But transgressing the rules too blatantly would be courting disaster no matter what you are selling or how important your company is back home.

NOTES

1. For broader studies of Japanese management skip "pop" works by American academics like *The Art of Japanese Management* and *Theory Z*, and try some books by Japanese specialists. Examples are Keitaro Hasegawa, *Japanese-Style Management*, Shuji Hayashi, *Culture and Management in Japan*, Kazuo Koike, *Understanding Industrial Relations in Japan*, and Toyohiro Kono, *Strategy & Structure of Japanese Enterprises*.
2. Even supposedly hard-headed businessmen like James and Jeffrey Morgan wax poetic about loyalty, harmony, etc. in *Cracking The Japanese Market*.
3. There are literally dozens of books on Japanese productivity, quality control, and other techniques. Two of interest are Sheridan M. Tatsuno, *Created in Japan*, and Masaaki Imai, *Kaizen*.
4. For further details on the inefficiency of white-collar employees and management in general, see Woronoff, *Japan's Wasted Workers*.

4

Choosing The Right Vehicle

There are two basic facts about the Japanese market that
nobody seems to question. The Japanese market is one of the
most attractive in the world. It is also one of the toughest in
the world. Depending on whether the pull or push is greater,
you should decide on how to approach doing business there.
But you should certainly not be put off by its toughness and
what you regard as your inability to crack it. There is more
than one way of getting in and some of the ways are much
less exacting than others.

The various entry points are discussed here, starting with
the simpler ones like exporting, licensing and franchising.
These are routes that are open to the smallest of companies
with an interesting product or service and which wants to
leave the hard part to Japanese agents. Next in line is joint
venturing, which makes considerably greater demands on the
foreign partner but still leaves major, usually more unfamiliar,
functions to a Japanese partner. Going it alone by setting up
a wholly owned operation is the most challenging, and sometimes most rewarding, alternative.[1]

Foreign companies should pick the vehicle which they think
meets their needs and for which they have adequate resources.
A joint venture or wholly owned subsidiary is more costly
not only in time but also money. It may take some while,
and considerable expense, to justify it. Just exporting, licensing or franchising can be arranged much faster and the returns

materialize more quickly. However, the bigger rewards will still probably flow to those making the bigger effort.

So, it is also a question of commitment. Companies which are strongly committed to the Japanese market will choose the latter alternatives, even if they initially start with the former. But that does not mean that companies with less commitment must necessarily be excluded, as some supposed "experts" insist.

In the discussion of the various vehicles, the reader will soon notice that there are not only advantages but drawbacks to each. That is not quibbling. Nor is it a subtle warning. This is not a question of absolutes but tradeoffs. Once you have decided to go ahead, you must weigh the pros and cons to determine which is the best compromise. If you are looking for pat formulas or ideal solutions, you should try another book.

Just Exporting

Exporting is a fairly standard, comparatively straightforward approach. It is not mentioned in most books on doing business in Japan, whose authors prefer more heroic endeavors. Still, it meets the basic requirement of selling your product in a market where there may be a demand and where success, even relative success, can be quite rewarding.

Of course, to enhance any chances of success, it is helpful to carefully choose the product. Some companies have only one. But others possess an array and one may do considerably better than the rest. This can be ascertained by market research, whether based on a reading of trade publications, visit to Japan, or full-blown study undertaken by a local consulting office. It would be wise to consider whether slight modifications in the product might not adapt it more to local conditions and thereby further increase sales potential.

Choosing the product is the first step. The second, frequently the most fateful one, is choosing the agent. For, once you have contracted a Japanese agent, most of the other steps will be taken by it, namely the choice of local distributors and outlets, pricing, positioning, advertising and so on. You may be able to offer advice, but don't count on it being followed to the letter. Moreover, since the agent knows the market so much better than you, don't be overly certain that you are right or it is wrong.

There are two basic options, general trading companies (*sogo shosha*) and specialized trading companies (*senmon shosha*). You should decide between them on the basis of the type of product, prospective sales, degree of technical know-how required, extent to which you want feedback, and so on.

The general trading companies or *sogo shosha* are best known abroad.[2] They get most of the publicity, both of their own making and articles by impressionable journalists and academics. After all, they are truly gigantic, with billions of dollars of annual turnover, thousands of employees, enormous financial resources and offices spanning the globe. While there is some specialization, they are amazingly diversified carrying literally thousands of different products from Japan to dozens of foreign countries and the other way around.

While most of the literature stresses their export prowess, they also import huge amounts of goods into Japan. In fact, imports account for more of their turnover than do exports and they control about a fifth of total wholesaling volume. In Japan, they have associates and subsidiaries which process many raw materials, manufacture assorted articles, or engage in distribution of goods. On the whole, they emphasize bulk products, including raw materials and other commodities, but they also handle large capital goods and larger consumer items as well as some services.

That means a *sogo shosha* may be suitable for your purposes. However, before even approaching one, remember that these large and variegated entities may not provide customized service which meets your needs. In addition, they will not even bother with your products unless a (rather large) minimum turnover can be expected. And, on the whole, they are somewhat less specialized than their smaller counterparts.

If a general trading company seems appropriate, you can usually start looking for one without even leaving home. You can contact the local JETRO office, which has directories providing information about the nine *sogo shosha* and their activities and will help you decide which is strongest in your line of business. You could then perhaps visit the trader's local office, since they have so many. If there is none conveniently located, you could write to the head office in Tokyo for an initial approach. If the prospects are interesting, someone will be sent to visit you. If not, as they say, ''don't call us, we'll call you.''

If your product is rather complicated, you need more customized service, you can only sell a limited amount or your company is fairly small, you are probably better off with a specialized trading company or *senmon shosha*. It will be able to meet your needs better and, being a small company itself, is unlikely to lord it over you. But it will still want to know that your product is promising, that there is a potential market, and that it can distribute the article properly. These are exactly the same questions you should be asking yourself. For, this time, with 10,000 *senmon shosha,* there is an enormous field to choose from and you have to get it right.

These smaller traders vary tremendously amongst themselves in exact specialization, size and financial strength, access to distributors and end-users and also ability to work with foreigners. Moreover, some are just traders and pass goods on to wholesalers while others are actually wholesalers with an international dimension. In the list are several foreign firms, which may for that reason be more adapted to handling foreign products. They include Dodwell, Jardine, and Gadelius.

Finding the right importer will take some effort, but it is time and money well spent. First, you might make a call to the nearest JETRO office or send a letter to your embassy or chamber of commerce in Tokyo to make recommendations. It will not be easy to choose without actually going there and meeting with the representatives of several traders. While in Japan, you should look more carefully into how similar products are handled and perhaps chat with foreign counterparts who know them to find out which traders they are using and what the results have been. Do not hurry the process. Take as much time as you need to find the right agent the first time.

So far I have referred to quite commonplace aspects of doing business, things you must be familiar with from experiences in other countries. However, as noted in the previous chapter, Japan is distinguished by particularly close relations between companies. So it is essential not only to determine whether a trader can do the job but whether it *will do the job*. That is, whether it may not make only half-hearted efforts due to a conflict of interest.

General trading companies are not only traders, they have subsidiaries which are manufacturers. If you produce the same thing as a subsidiary, they may not wish to deal with you at all or will give you second-rate treatment.[3] Some specialized traders are also manufacturers or, if not, they are very closely related to manufacturers. They may also prove unsuitable. This means it is indispensable to do some serious research into the web of relations to discover whether such conflicts exist and, if so, give your preference to agents which are not bound this way.

Licensing and Franchising

The Japanese market is very large. It is also very distant from most other countries. This means that it can be rather costly and also time-consuming to ship goods to Japan by sea or air. It may, under certain circumstances, be much cheaper to have them produced locally. That idea, by the way, is just as likely to occur to a Japanese company as the foreign one and, after considering the alternatives, they may decide that licensing is the best way to go.

The ideal partner for licensing, unlike exporting, is a manufacturer. But this time it is necessary to be even more selective. First, you have to check that the manufacturer can make the product competently and cheaply enough to sell locally. Then you have to determine whether it has access to suitable distribution channels. Finally, it is wise to find out if the product competes directly with one of its own or fills a gap. Your product does not have to be "unique," but it must round out the licensee's line if it is to receive strong support.

The situation for franchising is similar, except that it usually applies to services which could not be "exported" to Japan even if you wanted. You have to reproduce locally the same sort of establishment you have developed in your own country, one which is hopefully distinctive enough to attract Japanese customers. Since "foreignness" may actually be a key selling point, the possibilities are amazingly broad. In fact, franchising has been one of the most traveled and successful routes of late with entrants increasing from several dozen to several hundred. They include all the big names and some small, from McDonald's, Kentucky Fried Chicken and Seven-Eleven to France Croissant.

Still, to succeed here it is indispensable to find the right partner. This can be even more difficult than for manufacturing because it is not so easy to just hand over the plans and go ahead. You must be certain that the level of compliance with your instructions is adequate, not just once in a while through spot checks of franchises, but regularly from year to year, from location to location. On the other hand, you may have to adjust your own procedures even more to suit local tastes without, however, losing the crucial elements that make your operation distinctive.

The possible range of partners is somewhat wider. You can choose a counterpart, a department store for boutiques, another retailer for special convenience stores, a food processor or distributor for fast food outlets, and so on. You can then count on a certain degree of familiarity with the sector, enough basic expertise to get started, and access to personnel, etc. Given the high cost of land, the best partner may be a company with large land holdings. Or, due to their many ramifications, a *sogo shosha* may prove suitable.[4]

As for exporting, you want an associate who can not only do the job but will work hard at it. That is never easy to determine in advance. But a routine check on experiences of similar foreign firms and the relations with other Japanese companies is certainly in order.

Once again, a call to your local JETRO office, a look at the various directories, an examination of some of the trade publications, a letter to the embassy or foreign chamber may give you a pretty good idea of potential partners. Attending trade shows at home, or preferably in Japan, may establish contacts. But this is a sufficiently serious matter that you may want a consulting office to undertake studies. And you should personally visit, or send an appropriate mission to, Japan to meet with potential partners and negotiate a clear agreement with whichever appears best.

Among the other looser arrangements one might include what is glibly called "strategic alliances." They can involve almost anything from joint distribution, to joint production to joint research and development. What is truly interesting here is that the emphasis is switching from foreigners as the leaders to Japanese as equals or leaders. More and more, Japanese companies are coming up with products that foreigners would like to license. They are also engaging in advanced research, the results of which foreign companies would like to acquire. In some cases, they may find it best to get in at the ground floor through co-development.[5]

Joint Venturing

Exporting, licensing and franchising are acceptable alternatives in their own terms. You export your products to Japan, as you do for Canada or France, and you get paid. You have your products manufactured in Japan and, in return for the specifications, instructions and rights, you get a royalty. You entrust your system to a Japanese franchisee and you receive mutually agreed fees. All this is very simple and straightforward. No hassle. No fuss. No need to figure out a complicated distribution network, bother with finicky clients or haggle with government officials. You don't even have to learn how to bow or use chopsticks.

But this is still a fairly low level of commitment. The returns are certainly attractive, but only commensurate with the input. Perhaps, if you did a bit more, the returns would be larger. Also, by upgrading your effort, you would certainly have more control over the operation. You would know who your customers are, what their requirements are, whether they are satisfied with your product or service. You would have more feedback. Also, from this level, it is rather hard to expand aside from entrusting more products or services to your agent or associate.

To increase control, enhance feedback, provide a basis for further growth, many foreign companies prefer taking an additional step. But they do not want to go it alone in a strange country they do not quite fathom. They prefer the alternative of a joint venture. Until the 1980s, they did not have much choice since investment was restricted. Now, despite the fact that 100% ownership is permitted, many still prefer this halfway house.[6]

This is justified by the ''tough market'' part of our equation. Some of the things that are particularly difficult about Japan include recruiting personnel, managing along Japanese lines and just buying or renting premises, given the exorbitant prices. But nothing seems harder than penetrating the distribution system. Finding the right channels, and then convincing the distributors to carry your products, can be such a daunting task that it puts off many otherwise eager businessmen.

Through a joint venture, the foreign company can share any efforts with a Japanese partner. The foreign side contributes the product, usually a rather special one in terms of price, quality or performance (if not quite unique). It grants the rights and passes on the technologies. It also shares the financial burden. The Japanese side usually provides the rest of the finance, access to distribution channels, and perhaps manufacturing facilities. It may also "loan" the initial staff, supply premises and deal with the government.

Choosing the partner for a joint venture is a much more delicate matter than picking an importer or licensee. It is necessary to find another company that can get the job done, and do it in a way you thoroughly approve of since closer cooperation is inevitable. Since you will be sharing an office, sometimes also a factory, and staff, the degree of compatibility must be much greater. Also, your partner should make its very best efforts to sell the goods produced. So you cannot afford a conflict of interest, i.e. having a partner with close relations to one of your competitors or which itself produces something too similar.

Moreover, in the Japanese context, a joint venture is a very serious relationship, more comparable perhaps to an old-fashioned marriage where both sides must stick together through good and hard times. That derives from customs and traditions. It is enforced by the need to "save face," something that acutely concerns any Japanese company but should also interest you if your intention is to show deeper commitment and seek long-term benefits.

For many years, a joint venture was not only the best way to participate actively, it was the only way due to restrictions on investment. Yet, even now, many foreigners like it. If you establish one, you will be in good company along with leading joint ventures like Fuji Xerox, Nihon Unisys, Sumitomo 3M, Yamatake-Honeywell, McDonald's Japan, Toppan Moore, DuPont Toray, etc., etc. But this vehicle is losing some of its luster.

In fact, there is presently a lively debate about the future of joint ventures. They are no longer imposed and some of what they offered can be obtained in other ways. More to the point, many were mediocre successes and some were outright failures. The explanation may be that, as was noted by Jackson N. Huddleston, Jr., a perceptive businessman and consultant, "many joint ventures have been shotgun weddings; neither side got what it wanted. The Japanese wanted a licensing agreement and the foreigner, especially Americans, wanted a wholly owned subsidiary."[7] Still, as he conceded, joint ventures continue to be formed to reduce costs or access distribution. Even today, the joint venture remains the principal form of cooperation.

This means that foreign companies should not only consider the possible advantages but any conceivable drawbacks and make every effort to avoid them. Much has been written on what goes into making a successful joint venture. Some of the better advice has come from Mark Zimmerman, who ran several during his years in Japan. Here are some of the factors he regarded as crucial.

"First, there must be a definite product, technology, marketing system, or brand that the partnership can immediately and profitably develop and exploit. Second, the Western firm must have a clear understanding with the Japanese partner regarding short-, medium- and long-range objectives and profit expectations. Third, the foreign partner has to be prepared for a relatively long payout period, and to accomodate this fact in its calculations when establishing financial objectives. Fourth, the foreign partner must remember that the Japanese look upon a joint venture as more than a simple business arrangement. They will view it just as they do their relationships with suppliers, distributors, agents or trading companies—as a relationship of trust that is expected to endure the test of time.''[8]

Going It Alone

Many foreign companies are worried about possible conflicts of interest and do not really trust Japanese counterparts. They may also hold proprietary rights to truly exceptional technologies they do not want to part with, not even to a carefully chosen partner. In some instances, the management philosophy emphasizes going it alone in all markets, domestic and overseas, and growing a venture from a small beginning rather than starting with a full-fledged one.

In such cases, a wholly owned subsidiary is certainly preferred. What is more, it is increasingly easy to arrange in Japan aside from very few sectors. This, however, means that the foreign company is saddled with certain problems a joint venture can avoid or at least simplify. They include the need to establish your own office, recruit your own personnel, handle your own distribution, subjects that will be dealt with in greater detail elsewhere. The financial demands are also greater. In return, any rewards should be that much larger because they do not have to be shared with a partner. That is another reason why the wholly owned venture beckons.

Yet, even if you take this route, it is possible to advance step by step. The very first step could be to set up a representative office. This could be a rather small, if fairly well-appointed (and expensive) office, with only one or two expatriates and some secretaries. It might do little more than follow events in the sector to know what your competitors are doing and give advance warning of new products or strategies.

Such an operation would be yet more useful if it kept an eye on your importers and distributors, to see how good a job they are doing and increase the feedback. This should obviously not just be filed. It should be used to encourage greater efforts on their part, since they know you are watching. It could also be used advantageously to adapt your products to customer wishes.

This office could also seek additional products which might then be exported to or produced in Japan. Most larger companies have a whole array and the first one they tried may not even have been the best. With a local operation, it is much easier to undertake appropriate market research to find the right product. It could also get a much better feel for the appropriate distributors and probably negotiate better conditions.

The next phase might be a branch office or actual subsidiary. Its initial focus could be improving distribution. This might involve adding new distributors to the old (or more rarely replacing them) so as to cover a broader territory. You could perhaps provide greater backup in terms of point-of-sale material or advertising. It would already be a much bigger step if you were to create your own distribution network, but one certain companies eventually find necessary. Other major strides would be to go over to local manufacturing and conceivably research and development.

All of these things are much, much, much easier said than done. And there will be times when you wish you had a partner. But, if you really want to become an active player and more of an insider, you must make the effort. This is a high stakes game, but the route requiring the biggest commitment also offers the greatest potential.

How you set up a corporation is something much better

discussed with a lawyer or judicial scrivener (*shiho shoshi*). But it should be mentioned in passing that the more formal "stock company" known as *kabushiki kaisha* or K.K. is not the only alternative. It is also possible to establish a limited liability company known as *yugen-kaisha* or Y.K. Helene Thian suggested the latter for small businesses, since it is easier to adopt and requires fewer formalities. She also opts for the scrivener as cheaper than a lawyer.[9]

While not yet a majority, wholly owned operations are increasingly popular and accessible. This category boasts many of the big names like IBM, Coca-Cola, Esso, Nestle, Digital Equipment, Intel, Hoechst and BMW. But there are also legions of tiny ventures, often launched by a single foreigner, who is out there on his own. Like the one I ran, they have to make up for size with speed and they cannot afford to wait for the Japanese side to come to a decision on every detail.

Consultants

This is a good point to return to an intermediary that was already mentioned in passing several times, the consultant. A consulting office in Japan can accomplish many useful tasks for the newcomer and even companies which are long established. The right one can smooth over so many difficulties and open so many doors that it can spell the difference between success and failure. If you get stuck with the wrong one, you would be much better off alone.

As already noted, a consulting office can do some essential basic research. It can, first of all, undertake market research itself or through a more specialized company in order to know more exactly the prospects for your product, how it should be marketed, what distributors should be used, and so on. It can check on your competitors to see whether they have similar products and how theirs compare. Even more important, it can participate actively in the search for suitable importers, licensees, franchisees or joint venture partners.

To establish the formal relations, a consultant can be particularly useful. It could fulfill the function of go-between in a society where even couples who have known one another for years want a go-between to officiate at their marriage. It is much easier for a consultant not only to seek a partner but to introduce you to such a partner, acting on your behalf but still more or less as a third party. It can then advise you on how to negotiate a deal, what conditions might prove acceptable, how to behave and so on. If the negotiations drag on, and you have to return home, it is important to have someone around who can follow up. While good news will be readily forthcoming, it may be easier for the consultant to coax out any bad news.

If you opt for exporting, licensing or franchising, you may not feel it is worthwhile establishing even a small permanent office. A consultant's office can probably do some of the follow-up, either by assigning a dedicated staff member or working on a case-by-case basis. Should you go further and set up an office, you may wish to locate it in a corner of the consultant's suite or have an outside one operated by the consultant. If you go ahead with a larger project, be it a joint venture or wholly owned subsidiary, the consultant can at least provide advice on where to find premises, what the going rates are, etc. If you want to recruit personnel, it could help find them or suggest a head-hunter to aid you.

Since the consultant can be so important, it is essential to pick the right one. That is not easy. But it is certainly much easier than selecting Japanese partners. For most of the consultants are foreigners, or used to working with foreigners, whether specialists or retired businessmen. You will at least find no great culture gap. You can also more readily get information on their previous experiences by checking with the embassy, foreign chamber or other foreign businessmen.

Conditions are fairly standard and rates can be negotiated. This may evolve into a long relationship but it can also be restricted to certain periods or services.

Still, it should not be forgotten that consultants—even when under contract with and paid by you—can have personal interests that do not entirely coincide with yours.

For one, they tend to prefer companies which keep a lower profile and do not set up a local office because then they are much more dependent on the consultant for information, advice and other paid services. If you wish to upgrade your operation, they may well suggest a joint venture rather than a wholly owned operation because you would again be in greater need of backup for a longer time. Probably the last thing they would do is tell you to give up on Japan. No, they will suggest alternative products, partners, approaches to keep you around and in their clientele.

That is all comprehensible. Consultants do the same thing everywhere. In Japan, there is a further wrinkle. Some consultants have greater affinity to certain Japanese companies or groups than others. Given the difficulty in establishing relations, they might steer you toward those they are familiar with. Alas, they may not be the right ones. So, it is best you check whether the consultant tends to favor the same source for tie-ups and, more important, whether this is indeed a suitable partner for you. That must be through your own sleuthing or the work of another consultant.

Pointers on Partnering

In connection with all of the various alternatives, there are certain strategic factors which should never be forgotten. They were occasionally hinted at but certainly deserve more specific treatment and, if necessary, repetition. All of them tie up with the concept of ''partnering'' which I hear endlessly. Foreign businessmen are busily seeking partners to import, distribute, license, franchise, manufacture, cooperate on research, etc. The ultimate form of partnership is apparently the joint venture.

Personally, I do not like the expression. I think it is not only misplaced, it can actually be misleading and get you in trouble if you assume the Japanese understand it in the same way as *gaijin*. Actually, the Japanese have no special liking or predisposition for such an arrangement. Partners are related in an often rather loose manner; the Japanese prefer stricter, more structured, relationships. Partners can be changed from time to time; the Japanese seek long-term associations. Above all, partners are roughly equal, no matter how big or important one may be compared to another. This clashes with the Japanese hang for hierarchy.

Another problem is that "partnering" has a warm, mushy, emotional quality, what the Japanese call "wet." This is supposed to involve more than just doing business together. There is an element of common challenge plus a note of possible friendship. No matter how much the Japanese fancy "wet" relationships and love to drink, chat and sing *karaoke* songs even with *gaijin* guests, it would be unwise to assume that they are partners, let alone friends. The relationship is strictly business and letting emotional overtones arise only deludes and weakens the foreign side.

Yet, foreign businessmen are constantly creating partnerships, many of which they are later surprised to find were not only flimsy but worked against them. Their Japanese partners, despite all the talk of "trust" and "human relations," failed to provide the inputs expected, reneged on agreements about prices or profits, and dillydallied on virtually everything. Worse, in some cases they copied the product and dumped the provider. That is certainly not how a partner should act!

Well, if they did not want this to happen, the *gaishi* should have thought about it earlier and taken appropriate precautions. Some, actually rather few, can be written into the contract. The others must be enforced by keeping an eye on the partnership and reminding the Japanese side of what is expected. This means not leaving too many decisions to your partner and looking for alternatives if things should sour. But much of this could be obviated if foreign companies reflected seriously on a few crucial points when picking partners.

For one, should you choose a partner who is in the same business or not? Obviously, for reasons of effectiveness, the former is more attractive. You will cooperate with another company which has experience in your sector, has distributors used to working there, knows how to produce your line of goods, and so on. Alas, this means it could conceivably clone your product and get along without you one of these days. Cooperation with a distributor, manufacturer or other company in another sector, while more complicated, may be safer.

So far, the vast majority of tie-ups were between likes: automaker with automaker, pharmaceutical firm with pharmaceutical firm, food processor with food processor, and so on. But one of the most significant success stories is Schick, which has its razor blades distributed through a company in the watch business. Other examples are Allstate Life Insurance whose policies are sold in Seibu's stores and Whirlpool which has its refrigerators distributed by Sony.

The second strategic choice is whether to work with a large, prestigious company or a smaller one. Again, the first is more appealing. It has a grander reputation, greater resources, broader distribution network, firmer government contacts, etc. Yet, this is the kind of partner which not only could dominate you, in a hierarchical society it may almost inevitably do so. Perhaps you would be better off with a company more your size or even smaller, one you could conceivably dominate.

The third question is whether to cooperate with a group or *keiretsu* as an "honorary" member of sorts by tying up with one of its participants. There are definite advantages, and they should not be underestimated. This would almost automatically open up sales possibilities. It would also make it easier to come by financing, obtain reliable suppliers and so on. The flip side is that, once within one group, it would be impossible to penetrate others. It might thus be best to remain outside although initially it will be harder to get by.

These are the three strategic decisions which must be made when picking a ''partner.'' All too often, they are overlooked by newcomers who stumble into arrangements which will influence their whole future and are extremely hard to reverse. I will not prejudge the answers. They should depend on the requirements of the foreign side and, as noted, there are pluses and minuses both ways. But at least do not forget about them in the hustle and bustle of getting into Japan.

At any rate, since relations with Japanese ''partners'' are of such consequence, it is essential to make them as positive as possible. It is therefore worthwhile considering the views of one businessman who has thought long and hard about the subject. That is T.W. Kang whose ''guidelines for a successful partnership'' follow:

''Balance global and local motives for partnering. Pick a compatible partner. Negotiate hard for return, but only in the context of a positive relationship for both parties; and structure the relationship properly. Commit the necessary resources to the execution of the partnership. Accept differences in culture. Develop credibility on both sides. Follow established principles of management. Keep contacts at high levels. Anticipate problems. Be flexible and willing to adjust.''[10]

NOTES

1. For further background on the various vehicles, see Czinkota and Woronoff, op. cit., pp. 141–75.
2. The nine *sogo shosha,* listed by turnover, are C. Itoh, Mitsui, Marubeni, Mitsubishi, Sumitomo, Nissho Iwai, Toyo Menka, Nichimen, and Kanematsu-Gosho. For general background on the operation of trading companies, see Max Eli, *Japan, Inc.*
3. To check the links between the general trading companies and the *keiretsu,* see Dodwell, *Industrial Groupings in Japan.*
4. See Michael G. Brennan and Daniel G. Lawton, ''The Right Partner and Structure for Franchising in Japan,'' *Venture Japan,* Vol. 2, No. 2.
5. On how this works in the pharmaceutical sector, see Reed Maurer, *Competing in Japan,* pp. 106–24.
6. For practical tips on how joint ventures operate, by executives who participated in them, see Huddleston, op. cit., T.W. Kang, *Gaishi,* Reed Maurer, op. cit., Morgan and Morgan, op. cit., and Zimmerman, op. cit.
7. Huddleston, op. cit., p. 121.
8. Zimmerman, op. cit., p. 232.
9. For some of the nuts and bolts of incorporation, taxation, etc., see Takashi Kuboi, *Business Practices and Taxation in Japan,* and Thian, op. cit.
10. Kang, op. cit., pp. 215–7.

5
Negotiating That Deal

On reading many of the popular books on doing business in Japan, and more particularly those on negotiating with the Japanese, you would think this is not the 1990s but the 1850s when Japan was just being opened. You are not a rather ordinary businessman come to sell widgets but Commodore Perry, who has arrived with his "black ships" on these inhospitable shores. And the Japanese are not equally ordinary businessmen out to buy widgets but the Shogun's retainers who hardly know what a foreigner is and certainly do not like dealing with one.

No. This really is the 1990s. By now, most foreigners have some idea of what Japan is all about and they should at least know the ramifications in the widget industry. They are negotiating with Japanese who have not only seen many foreigners, they have probably traveled abroad and quite conceivably know more about your country than you do about theirs. You are not the first foreigner they have dealt with. Indeed, they have dealt with many more foreigners than you with Japanese. And, despite any difficulties, both sides are interested in reaching a deal on widgets.

Keep this in mind when you read the books or see the video tapes that supposedly prepare you to negotiate with those wily Japanese. Don't believe anything too far-fetched or exotic. Don't assume that things will be entirely different (although much will be). And remember that adapting too much to the Japanese can be as perilous, probably more so, than not going far enough.

Know Thyself First

Most primers on negotiating start with the Japanese side. I much prefer starting with the foreign side. What *you* do is not only just as important, it will probably be much more decisive. So it does not hurt to examine your position and what the implications are.

First of all, as for any negotiations anywhere, you must consider your product and whether it should appeal to your counterpart. If you have done some market research, you should know whether the product will prove popular or not. You may also know whether the other side wants it badly, or less so, because it has something similar. You might even know whether it needs your product to compete with Japanese rivals.

Depending on this analysis, you can determine whether to make more or less stringent demands regarding price, payments, delivery, protection or proprietary rights, control of third markets, and so on. That is what you do everywhere, so why not in Japan? The only difference is that, in Japan, having the upper hand should be used to the best advantage and not frittered away. Don't assume that we are all in the same boat together and wouldn't it be nice to make things easy for my new partner. The Japanese side would probably not do the same if the situation were reversed.

If it turns out, unfortunately, that your product is not that exceptional, that there are some technical or commercial hitches, that there are competing products in Japan, let alone with your counterpart, you can expect much rougher sailing. You will have to come down on your price, guarantee improved quality and delivery, be less strict on who sells where and so on. You will have much less leverage and not knowing it or not acting on it will only make you look presumptuous and result in longer, more painful negotiations.

Knowing yourself goes a bit further in Japan because of hierarchy. Most foreign businessmen work on the assumption, one that is quite widespread in the West, that both parties are equal and being smaller or larger has little to do with negotiating. It is the product, price, conditions, etc. which count. That does not wash in Japan. (It may not even be entirely true in the West.) Bigger companies are much higher up the social ladder than smaller ones. They can have greater pretensions and expect token concessions for this reason alone. Remember that if you represent a small company. On the other hand, if you are the larger of the two, take advantage of it. Not doing so may assuage your counterpart's worries, but it will not enhance respect in any way.

Going somewhat further toward Japaneseness, it should be noted that sellers and buyers are most definitely not on an equal footing. Sellers, in the Japanese context at least, are lesser beings and they are expected to play up to the buyers. Buyers not only can but do make considerable demands of every sort, quality, delivery, service and price. This being understood, it would be unwise to start with conditions that are already so good they cannot be improved enough to satisfy the buyer, assuming you are the seller. If you are the buyer, once again, you would be unwise to go easy on your counterpart as this might induce contempt more than relief.

These points should be seriously considered before negotiating with the Japanese. The rules are fairly strict and hard to avoid. Moreover, they can play into your hands as well if you know what you are doing. But it is not necessary to go much further in trying to fit in.

Books on doing business in Japan are full of suggestions on how you can become a surrogate Japanese. They explain how you should talk, how you should dress, how you should look at people. They then go on to indicate conversational gambits to show just how much you respect the Japanese nation, the company and its products, how you admire their efforts and achievements. To this is added tips on how to go drinking with them, what cultural or sports events to attend (and report on to your counterparts), and where to eat. But much of this is superfluous and you will not get much more mileage out of altering your external appearance or personality than being yourself.

Not only is it insulting to foreigners to suggest that they should imitate Japanese practices and ape Japanese behavior, it is pointless. No matter how hard they try, they will never pull it off. And it is not at all certain that the Japanese want them to "go native." They usually feel more comfortable with *gaijin* who behave as such. Of course, you should be on your best behavior, you should make the best possible appearance, and you should be agreeable. More than that is not really appropriate.

Indeed, going much further is an insult to the Japanese. It assumes that they will be influenced by your artificial bowing and scraping, your feigned interest in things Japanese, your futile attempts to adapt to them. After all, these are seasoned businessmen who have negotiated numerous deals. They are looking for the best product, delivery and price just like any intelligent businessmen. Your appearance will make some difference, but the quality of your product will be much more decisive. So, do your utmost there and leave cultural fun and games to others.[1]

Give . . . and Take

Whole books have been written on negotiating with the Japanese.[2] Many include extensive case histories. Not everything they say is useful, but much is. So there is no point in trying to reproduce this in a short essay. Still, it is worthwhile referring to several salient points, including some where the "experts" have gone wrong.

First of all, Japanese negotiations are considerably more formal than in the West, although no more so than in many other Oriental countries. Meetings will be held in fine rooms, sometimes located in a posh hotel. Participants on the Japanese side will turn out dressed for the occasion in a well-cut if sober suit. They will also speak more formally. It would be appropriate for the foreign side to go along with this taste for formality, without overdoing it. Westerners can be more simply dressed but would be unwise to drop their jackets, talk loudly or crack too many jokes. No need to warn the Orientals, they already know.

The negotiating table will not be as long as the one in Versailles, but it will have to be rather long to accomodate the Japanese team which will be fairly numerous. The Japanese participants will be seated according to rank, from top executives to lower-level employees and "bag carriers." You could probably tell them apart anyway thanks to seniority. The older are likely to be the more exalted. Senior members, by the way, may only be around for opening and closing sessions, leaving juniors to conduct actual business. Once a (positive) conclusion has been reached, the chairman or some such will appear to sanction it.

The foreign team will probably be smaller, whether because it is expensive to send people to Japan or because top executives have greater decision-making powers. There is no need to apologize for this or feel uncomfortable. You should only take those who really are needed, bringing more bodies serves little purpose. But you might round out the team with a local advisor or consultant. As much as possible, the foreigners should be seated opposite Japanese of roughly the same rank or function, although it may bemuse the Japanese to see the age gaps.

In addition to formal sessions, there will be much wining and dining, some of it pretty lavish. That is supposed to create a cordial atmosphere and allow participants to meet one another more informally. For the Japanese, who like one-on-one relations, it may be a chance to get to know you. It may also be an opportunity to find out more about you and your prospects. You should also get to know them, and more about them, since informal contacts may produce more useful feedback than formal ones. For that, of course, you must listen more than you talk, a point too often forgotten by Westerners.

During the negotiations, present your proposals as simply and unambiguously as possible. Also provide plenty of written documentation. This is partly for linguistic reasons since many Japanese who cannot speak English fluently can read it. In addition, they have a passion for the printed word. They love to collect facts and figures and if any are missing you can expect questions at the next session.

In answering such questions, and presenting oral or written material, accuracy is another imperative. The Japanese will surely have done their homework and will know whether you are sticking to facts or embroidering. The latter would not be well received and could indispose them toward closer cooperation. By the way, after answering the first barrage of questions, you can expect a second and third.

Whatever happens, don't be intimidated or rattled by the questions. Some are put to obtain necessary information. Others are really intended to soften you up and get you on the defensive so that you will lower your demands. At the same time, don't forget to ask purposeful and probing questions of the Japanese. After all, if they have the right to know that your product is good, you have the right to find out whether they can distribute or manufacture it properly. There has been far too much ''overpromising'' by trading companies and others to simply assume that they can do all the things they claim.

Alas, as you must know by now, you will receive stilted presentations from the Japanese plus proposals of a sort.

They will be neither simple, nor unambiguous nor (sometimes) overly precise. The Japanese tendency toward indirect language, equivocating statements, responses that can be understood in different, even contrary manners, is already legendary. So it may take you some time to know just what the other side wants, let alone whether you can comply with it.

Equally well known is that negotiations may drag on much longer than elsewhere, whether in the West or the NICs, and appear quite inconclusive until a decision is finally reached. There are various reasons for this. Some, but only some, have been explained by the cross-cultural communicators.

For one, as noted in Chapter 3, the Japanese tend to work in groups and decisions are only reached after consulting all and sundry. It is necessary to have everybody on board and this can involve lots of *nemawashi*. Since this cannot be done during negotiations, there will be repeated calls for recess or further invitations for entertainment (which leaves them free to sort things out). That is legitimate, sort of. But the delay may also be due to hesitation on the Japanese side. They may not really want to do the deal and prefer stalling to conceding this. Worse, it may be tactical. Perhaps they do not want to do a deal with you, but they don't want you to go to another Japanese firm instead. Thus, the negotiations are kept in limbo.

It is vital to determine what the cause is since your response should differ. If it is only for *nemawashi* but otherwise things are proceeding well, give them more time. If they are just stalling because they don't like the terms, try to draw that out in private from someone you know fairly well and may talk informally. Then adjourn and decide whether you can modify your position. If there really is no hope (and here you will not get much help from Japanese ''friends''), start looking for alternative solutions.

Since delay can mean so many things, don't jump to conclusions. But don't let the negotiations drag on forever either. How hard you push for an agreement should depend less on tactics than knowing yourself. If this deal is very important to you, wait longer and if need be make concessions. If it is less important, withdraw politely. If you think you could do well enough with another Japanese company, get into contact with it. I know, the "experts" will tell you that it is improper to negotiate with more than one Japanese partner. But you must have a fallback position and that knowledge might hasten the negotiations.

When you finally do reach a deal, you had better confirm very precisely what it is. This is necessary because of the imprecision of the Japanese language which has relatively few ways of saying "no" and countless ways of saying "yes" but meaning something considerably less than that. Ask some questions and get some specifics on how the Japanese intend to fulfill their side of the agreement. If you can get this in writing, so much the better.

More Dos and Don'ts

There are plenty of other dos and don'ts I could mention. Like don't bore the Japanese with tales of your wife and kids and dog and house in the country and your war record although they are occasionally fascinated by your golfing exploits. Don't slurp your soup but, on the other hand, don't forget to slurp your *soba* as a sign of appreciation. Don't pass food from your chopsticks to somebody else's (that brings bad luck). Don't flirt with the girls serving tea or walk off with the hired hostess at the formal reception. But there are other sources for that.[3]

Rather, I would like to make some comments that are directed against the overall approach of many cross-cultural communicators who hold forth on the subject of negotiating with the Japanese. They have often gone a few steps too far.

Instead of merely presenting the Japanese way of doing things, they unjustifiably assume that it is *the* way that things should be done and imply that the best solution for *gaijin* is to adapt.

I disagree. If there is one basic rule about negotiating which should apply in all times and all places it is that it should meet the needs of both sides. It would be terribly foolish of you to let the Japanese have everything their way. If they want to be exceedingly formal, fine. If they want bloated negotiating teams, fine. You don't have to comply. If they want further details on your proposals, fine. Give it to them. If, on the other hand, they present their own proposals or respond to you ambiguously, not fine. Even if it makes the cross-cultural quibblers squirm, you have a right to demand further precision so you know what the situation really is.

In the same vein, it would be silly to swallow the Japanese line, since espoused by more "sensitive" foreign specialists, that the Japanese are not legalistic, contractual folks and thus an informal agreement is adequate. Maybe they are less legalistic with one another. With foreigners, it is quite a different case. According to one keen observer:

"Don't let anybody tell you Japanese don't like contracts. Don't let anybody tell you the Japanese don't read contracts. When you negotiate a contract with a Japanese you had better be sure what you are doing because they will live by every word in that agreement. Japanese are very legal minded when they are dealing with Westerners."[4]

What is somewhat closer to the truth is that the Japanese think less highly of contractual arrangements than Westerners do and they are also more eager to modify them to keep up with realities. In addition, they try to avoid actual litigation for reasons of "face" or other. In their eyes, "mutual discussion" (*hanashiai*) and conciliation are much better ways of settling disputes. Still, it is best to get something on paper. If nothing else, this helps both sides know just what has been agreed. In the event that there should be subsequent conflicts, it does not hurt to have a viable base for legal action.

I agree that legal action should not be a first resort. Indeed, the Japanese are situational and even the most legalistic foreigner must concede that the situation can change. So, if your partners subsequently want a revision, consider whether it is acceptable and, if it helps you less than them, get something in return. You can usually find a compromise. Conciliation is much nicer (and infinitely cheaper) than litigation. No harm in trying it. Not to do so would not only spoil your relationship with the other party, it would make it harder to do business in Japan. Still, if you remain aggrieved, the evidence on your side is strong, and you are not worried by fallout in Japan, call in the lawyers.

By the way, where negotiations are held can be almost as important as how they are conducted. The Japanese love to have *gaijin* come to Japan. It permits them to show off their headquarters and factories, invite participants to posh restaurants and bars, and create a climate which they assume is conducive to their own interests. In addition, they know how expensive it is to stay in a hotel and that the foreigners will eventually get bored and want to return home. This pressure could lead them to conclude a deal faster . . . and on less attractive terms. Meanwhile, the Japanese can consult with their experts, engage in all the *nemawashi* they want and determine exactly what sort of compromise is acceptable.

Two can obviously play this game. Why shouldn't the Japanese party make the trip to your head office, be invited to your home (admittedly a second-rate form of entertainment), and run up huge bills at the hotel. They might also come under pressure to hasten the proceedings. Alas, it is not that simple. Japanese are not as weak-kneed as *gaijin,* they will not give in just to reach a quick deal. Worse, they probably do not even have the authority to conclude one and must return home for another round of *nemawashi*. Then you may finally be invited back to Japan to sign the agreement.

One further point. Don't fall for the line, often pushed by supposed "experts," that Japanese negotiators are superlatively sly and subtle. That they are insidiously leading you into a trap that must inevitably result in their victory . . . unless you can be equally subtle. Thus, one popular book on Japanese negotiation is subtitled "subtlety and strategy beyond Western logic."[5] The cover is graced with a Japanese businessman dressed as a *ninja* and carrying a briefcase and sword.

Well, some Japanese negotiators are very tricky or devious. But most are reasonably businesslike. After all, they are not surrounding a castle or assassinating an evil lord. They are trying to buy, or sell, or market spark plugs, or corned beef or perfume. Uppermost in their minds are questions of quality, delivery, price and so on. True, there may be some deviousness involved if they are also calculating whether to go with you or stick with a local supplier, whether to help you or aid a group member, and so on. But most of their decisions are fairly rational.

They may also be fairly predictable if you have done your homework. This means that, rather than poring over the pages of *The Japanese Negotiator* or like books, you have been carefully studying the market so you know how your product compares on quality, delivery and price, so you know who in their group makes what, so you know if this is a tempting offer or one they can take or leave. If they want to take it, you will find them much less "subtle" and much more forthcoming. If they remain "subtle," it may be that the terms are not good enough. That, at least, is not an idea beyond Western logic.

Just two last don'ts while I'm at it. Don't give in to pleas made by Japanese businessmen, and endorsed by fuzzy foreign friends, that you place due emphasis on "human relations" (*ningen kankei*) and "trust" (*shinrai*). The appeal may be genuine. It could just as well be a ploy. What it may mean in practice is that you should make further concessions to reach an agreement. So, if you do give a little, try to get something back in the name of "human relations" and "trust."

And another ploy. Don't believe Japanese businessmen when they insist that you take the first step toward long-standing relations by offering exceptionally good conditions the first time around. They will probably not improve the conditions subsequently. If anything, the tendency is to make them ever stiffer. Moreover, there is absolutely no guarantee that you will have a second or third chance in which to recoup. They may just as well return to Japanese associates or other foreigners dumb enough to fall for the trick.

I say this with some discomfort since I was among the dumb foreigners to be taken in. I was also naive enough to believe most of the nonsense spread by supposed "experts." You should at least be forewarned. Then you can either reject these pleas or, better yet, shape your initial offer to accomodate possible concessions.

Language and Body Language

There is no question but that Japanese is a very complicated language. It is also a very ambiguous one. So you had better be able to cope with it. The best way is to get first-rate interpreters. There are not as many of those as one would like but they can be obtained, sometimes for an appreciable sum. Whatever the sum, if they do a good job it is worth every yen of it. If you do business frequently with the same company, try to bring along the same interpreter. It takes time to learn the relevant terminology and understand the technicalities of the subject. This consistency tends to reassure your Japanese counterparts as well.

It is definitely preferable to have *your* interpreter rather than one provided by your hosts. You can trust him or her more and you may get useful feedback. It is not only a question of words but how they are expressed and what may lie behind them, something that can be passed on during the recess. The interpreter may also be useful in filling you in on points of etiquette and procedure. But never forget that interpreting is a mere service and, no matter how interesting or charming the interpreter, you should focus attention on your Japanese counterparts at all times, during negotiations or social activities.

The interpreter's task is not an easy one given the complexities of the Japanese language and the ambiguity with which it is frequently used. So do what you can to facilitate it. On your side at least, speak clearly and simply and also keep to the point. Avoid unnecessary verbiage, going off on tangents or muttering. Don't toss in jokes or anecdotes or use colloquialisms that are hard to translate. If you do expect to use technical terms, it does not hurt to indicate them to the interpreter in advance so they can be looked up in a technical dictionary if need be.

You should speak in short but complete sentences. Competent interpreters can go sentence by sentence or in longer segments, so you might ask which is preferred. It may happen that the English (or other language) rendition of the Japanese appears a bit short. That may not be the interpreter's fault. The Japanese spokesman may have added lots of circumlocutions or hemmed and hawed. If, on the other hand, you feel that something is missing or awry, you can ask to have parts repeated. That is only natural.

The following suggestion is somewhat less natural. It might even qualify as ''subtlety and strategy beyond Japanese logic.'' Still, here goes. Your biggest problem is that the Japanese side will be ambiguous, that you will get answers that can be construed as yes or no, that even some technical specifications may be unclear. It is hard to pin the blame for this on the exalted Japanese businessman you are dealing with. But you can pretend that you did not quite get the drift, which you are sure can be traced to linguistic difficulties, and press for more precise answers.

This brings us to the question of speaking Japanese yourself rather than using an interpreter. There are now foreigners with an excellent command of the language and who, under ordinary circumstances, can get along quite nicely on their own. They could even negotiate deals. But, is it really in their interest? For then they would be stuck with equivocal answers and ambiguous conclusions. They could not really ask for clarification because that would either imply that their Japanese is inadequate or—far more embarrassing—that their opposite number is hard to comprehend. That is why many excellent Japanese speakers still use interpreters.

This being said, it is hard to grasp why some academics and cross-cultural quacks now urge foreign businessmen to study Japanese body language. Much fuss is also being made about nonverbal communication through *haragei* or "stomach language" where one's facial expression and gestures are expected to convey—even more deeply and effectively than words—one's true feelings. Whether this is so is open to question. Usually, it is impossible to read anything on the face of a Japanese interlocutor and the gestures are equally untranslatable. Often supposedly perceptive Japanese have trouble knowing what one another are thinking or expressing and, even in Japan, there has been a tendency to let this worthy tradition die.

Whatever the case, while the Japanese do still use *haragei* to some extent to fill the gaps and lapses in verbal communication, it is quite another matter to recommend that foreigners also apply it. Yet, assorted handbooks focusing on the cultural aspects of negotiating insist on the importance of body language and *haragei*. Well, if you cannot tell exactly what a Japanese is saying when he uses words, how can you—a mere *gaijin*—possibly guess his deeper meaning through facial clues or gestures? You are better off not even trying!

NOTES

1. Thian also suggests being yourself. "The advantage of being foreign is to use your 'foreignness,' meaning that you can be straightforward and get the answers because the Japanese will expect such behavior. Remember not to play either role, the ugly American (or other nationality) or the Japanized foreigner, bowing lower, eating more raw fish, and swigging more *saké* than your Japanese host." Thian, op. cit., p. 27.
2. On negotiating, to be taken sometimes with a grain of salt, see John L. Graham and Yoshihiro Sano, *Smart Bargaining*, Robert M. March, *The Japanese Negotiator*, Robert T. Moran, *Getting Your Yen's Worth*, and Rosalie L. Tung, *Business Negotiations With The Japanese*. On negotiating by a businessman, not an academic, see Zimmerman, op. cit., pp. 91–129.
3. On Japanese business etiquette, to be taken with two grains of salt, see Jon Alston, *The Intelligent Businessman's Guide to Japan*, Boye de Mente, *How To Do Business with the Japanese*, Alison R. Lainier, *The Rising Sun on Main Street*, and Diana Rowland, *Japanese Business Etiquette*.
4. Huddleston, op. cit., p. 89.
5. *The Japanese Negotiator* by March.

6

Getting Personnel

Many foreigners who have done business in Japan regard finding (and keeping) the right personnel as particularly difficult, perhaps the hardest task of all.[1] There you are, a stranger to this country, and you must assemble a team that will demonstrate ability and dedication so that the new company can grow. That is not easy anywhere. In Japan, you are faced with a different culture, different attitudes toward employment and a different employment system as such. There is also, and one should not hide it, a deep-rooted bias against working for foreign companies, especially if they are also small and new . . . which is usually the case at least initially.

To understand the problem, it helps to remember the brief description of lifetime employment in Chapter 3. Japanese companies recruit most of their employees straight from school and keep them until they retire. There is relatively little acquisition of mid-career staff and there are rather few candidates for such posts. In short, aside from the very young and the very old, there is not much choice. There is no labor market as commonly understood in the West or even most of Asia.

Nonetheless, you cannot run even the smallest operation without some staff. With a representative office, you may only need one or two persons. With a joint venture, the requirement could easily exceed a dozen. And if you intend to establish an active subsidiary, you may ultimately want considerably more. How then can you obtain enough staff, let alone a team of competent and committed employees who will hopefully strive for your success?

Recruiting Staff

Since you must have some staff somehow, you should naturally tap whatever resources exist. While comparatively limited, there is a small pool of mid-career personnel who can be hired to fill specific slots, accountants, clerical workers, factory workers, technicians, and so on. It is possible to advertise for them in the Japanese media, including English-language dailies which are more likely to produce results if you need linguistic abilities as well. There are also labor exchanges and notices can be posted in local towns if you have factories there.[2]

These turn out candidates. Many of them, you will soon realize, are part of an even smaller contingent of Japanese who willingly seek employment in *gaishi* and have probably already been through one or more. They have linguistic abilities, they usually have skills (indeed, more so than the average employee) and they can usually do the job. What is less certain is whether they will prove particularly loyal. Having left a Japanese firm, and then perhaps one or more foreign firms before coming to you, they may very well move on subsequently. Another problem is cost: they tend to gravitate toward the highest bidder.

There is another category of potential employees consisting largely of older Japanese, either retired or close to retirement age. They are seeking a post-retirement job that is better than what can be expected from their company and hope to find it with a foreign firm. They may well do so. But, if they could not get a good enough offer from their long-term, lifetime employer, they are unlikely to be among the best. They will be less demanding on wages but may have acquired rather few usable and transferable skills.

Repeated experiences with these categories of potential personnel will quickly lead you to the head-hunters and executive recruitment chaps. They are not hard to find and haunt the various chambers of commerce and foreigners' clubs. Actually, they are just as likely to find you. They do have long lists of potential personnel, and some of their candidates are doubtlessly a notch or two above what you have been getting through normal channels. They could conceivably come up with just the sort of people you want.

However, they will probably also be focusing on two categories, somewhat better than those mentioned but not entirely so. Most interesting are Japanese employees of Japanese companies who, since they are still working there, can be assumed to be relatively capable. Alas, given the closed nature of Japanese offices, this will be hard to ascertain. If they do come, they may not be the best. They may not have many specific skills but rather a profound knowledge of how their company works plus excellent connections. The question remains: can this be transferred to your own company and help it?

If such candidates are not available, the head-hunters will quickly turn to the other category of Japanese working for foreign companies. They are certainly more likely to be competent, since that is expected by such employers, and perhaps also more dynamic. They will at least have experience in dealing with *gaishi* if not necessarily the specific skills applicable to your own. But they may not be overly loyal and they could be rather costly. The trouble with both is that you will have to pay top yen to get them . . . and they could move on to the next, higher bidder in due course.

About now, you may be susceptible to an argument which has been cropping up with increasing frequency. Why not hire women? Obviously, in the above, I never mentioned the gender of the employees because in the Japanese context they could only have been males. Still, there are lots of women who are dynamic, eager to work and have just as good an education, or so the story goes. Alas, no matter what they say, many of them will still retire rather young, they may have gone to less rigorous schools and studied less useful subjects and, alas, dynamic women will frighten the stodgier men in your office out of their wits.

Here, it is not a question of being a male chauvinist so much as conceding existing Japanese realities. Many of the women who seek jobs will not work out for personal reasons or because of resistance from the male staff. Even if they are first-rate, and many certainly are, they may have to be largely restricted to tasks within the office rather than sent out to deal with customers or suppliers. And there could be friction if they rise through the ranks or waste if they are happy to remain "flowers of the office." This does not mean you should not employ them. It does suggest you do so more cautiously than in the West.

Another alternative, one which is becoming quite fashionable, is to recruit Japanese personnel not in Japan but abroad. They can be sought within the ranks of those pursuing advanced education, whether technical or management. These are often more skilled and versatile candidates, if they have come on their own (rather than being sent by their employer) they should also have more initiative, and they are more likely to blend into a *gaishi* than others. This solution was recommended by P. Reed Maurer, among others, who felt that "a deliberate program to search out these people can provide a cadre of talented middle managers in a relatively short time."[3]

As per usual, no solution is perfect and such staff may be more expensive than others. They may also have expectations that cannot be readily met. On the other hand, they will at least speak the language and could first work in the company's home office before being transferred to Japan, which would acquaint them with the products and personnel practices. Considering the alternatives, this is certainly a more promising option.

Obviously, while mulling over personnel, and figuring out what they are worth, you do have to get some work done. Thank goodness, by now there is a proficient temp industry with many local and some foreign firms (like Manpower) ready and willing to provide clerical, technical and even blue-collar staff on a temporary basis and at competitive rates. These people usually possess more skills since that is what they are selling on the market place. If they are not loyal, that does not really matter since you can phone for another. Not only will they get the work done, they will give you the time to evaluate candidates for regular employment rather than rushing into decisions which may prove hasty and costly.

However you ultimately do it, and whoever you ultimately hire, it must sadly be concluded that you will probably have a second (or third) rate staff by Japanese standards. You will not get the most able or best educated employees, the team you form will be quite mixed with regard to age, sex and previous experience, and you can only count on limited loyalty. Your operation could not possibly function as smoothly as those of your Japanese rivals. For this, you will be paying overgenerously. Your costs could easily be 20–30% higher, not counting the fact that employees may put in less overtime and insist on more perks and longer vacations.

Borrowing and Growing Staff

Given the unusual difficulty in recruiting staff, you may be receptive to an offer from a joint venture partner that it loan the necessary staff. After all, it has its own competent, loyal people who can be seconded to your joint operation under the *shukko shain* system. This will be a real team, with real executives, specialists and general staff. They will be able to function from the word go. They will also be paid the standard wage, much cheaper than a group of mercenaries.

This offer of "borrowing" staff has definite advantages. And it should not be rejected without carefully considering the alternatives. Can you really recruit a better, more effective and cheaper team on your own? Probably not.

But that does not mean that there are only pluses. One drawback is that your partner is unlikely to offer you the pick of the parent company's personnel. You will probably be getting less trained or experienced specialists, generalists who show less talent, and among the top executives some it wanted to get rid of anyway. As Thomas J. Nevins, a specialist on personnel, says: "No firm will loan you their best employees and chances are they are even one or two grades below average."[4] So, even if they are not paid more than other Japanese, if they are underaverage performers wages would still be on the high side.

However, all this pales compared to the real problem. These are employees who have worked their way up through the Japanese company, who may eventually return there, and who at any rate have considerable loyalty to it. If they form a complete team, aside from one or two foreigners, they will stick to their old ways rather than learn yours. They will be committed to the success of the joint ventures as long as it remains joint. However, if one day the partnership should dissolve, they will stick to the Japanese side and you will be left without a staff.

This means that, if you accept the option, you must make every effort to obtain the best possible personnel. You must insist on careful screening of those being transferred and the right to reject some of them later on if they do not work out. More important, you should participate in the decision-making to see if the managers are capable and have the same vision of the joint company. You cannot pick your counterpart, that is the prerogative of the Japanese side, so at least ensure that you have people you can work with at lower levels.

The third alternative to recruiting or borrowing staff is to grow it Japanese-style. That means taking in a new class of employees fresh from school each year. This method can be adopted both in joint ventures and wholly owned subsidiaries. In both cases, the newcomers will be trained by existing employees and will gradually move up over a period of many, many years as the older retire and are replaced by the home-grown lot. While referred to as an alternative, it is actually more of a complement to both since it takes thirty years to go through the whole process.

There are several notable advantages to this approach. The biggest, in Japanese eyes, is loyalty. These are personnel who expect to stay with the company throughout their career and are naturally dependent on its success. They will fight harder to make it succeed. They will also enter without preconceived notions of how a company should be run (hardly the case for mid-career or seconded staff) and could thus be more readily shaped. They will also eventually form a more homogenous team.

That is not to say that there are no disadvantages. The worst is temporary. It will be extremely difficult to create a proper interface between the fresh recruits and the older staff, whether hired individually or taken en masse from your partner. They will not have quite the same goals. They will not function in quite the same manner. And they may not even have the same pay and conditions. There could eventually be friction or jealousy among the older staffers who fear earlier than anticipated replacement.

The other headache, of course, is that it is not so easy to recruit graduates fresh out of school. You must first approach the school and convince the appropriate authorities or specific professors that your company is indeed a worthy employer, that it will treat whoever it recruits properly and, stickiest, that it is likely to be around during their career and well beyond. Even then, in the early years, you will only get a few candidates and they may not be the very best. Only gradually, as you become better known and those you already recruited begin recommending and persuading their juniors, will you get the sort of personnel you want.

Nonetheless, the general consensus among foreign managers with extensive experience in Japan is that this is the way to go. It may not be a feasible path at first. But somewhere along the line, if not company-wide than at least in bits and snatches, it is wisest to begin growing your own staff.

Sizing Up the Japanese

Whether you recruit them, borrow them or grow them, you will have to pick and choose among possible candidates. You will not only have to hire Japanese, you will have to hire the right ones. That is not easy for anyone, including other Japanese. It is particularly difficult for *gaijin,* only partly because they are unfamiliar with the culture and find it hard to evaluate individuals. That is not surprising, Japanese candidates are extremely good at selling themselves, they adapt to what they think you want almost chameleon-like and do their best to please.

So, you may be tempted to leave the selection to your Japanese colleagues. Certainly, they have a better feel for what their compatriots really think and seek and how they are likely to perform. They know what is on the market and how to separate the wheat from the chaff, or whatever. Alas, what they want may not be exactly what you want. And they may be moved by preconceived notions and biases that blind them to hidden virtues (at least in your eyes).

The best example is academic background, the primary screen most often. Japanese companies look for credentials, i.e. did the person graduate from a first, second or third-rate college? Did he come from prestigious Tokyo University, or more independent Keio and Waseda which turned out generations of business leaders, or some smaller or provincial school? They would tend, all things being equal, to pick someone from the better school even if his or her ability and knowledge were less. That is pure snobbishness in most cases. The person from the lesser school may be better and may also have to outperform to prove it.

But it is not just to show that you are not a snob that you may accept the lesser candidate. You cannot get people from top schools anyway and, if they do come, there may be something wrong with them. If the rest of your staff does not boast equivalent credentials, there is bound to be social friction. More important, if you are counting on academic credentials to succeed, you are destined to lose because you can never match larger Japanese companies. So, you have to look for something else.

One of the best things to look for is competence. Most Japanese candidates inducted into larger companies are pure generalists. In fact, too much specialization hurts their chances. With a smaller company, and less room for generalists to rise, you could do with more specialization. You also want people who think as opposed to having social graces. If they are a bit more dynamic, that does not hurt. Elsewhere, they would stand out like the proverbial nail that (in Japan at least) has to be hammered in. In a partly foreign venture, that will be noticed less.

Evaluating such people will not be simple. As noted, many of the mid-career types will have left (or lost?) their job with a Japanese company and perhaps moved from one foreign company to another. You have to figure out why. Are they incompetents, who just could not do the job? Are they malcontents, who could not stay put? Or are they talented individuals whose skills were not being rewarded? Did they just get tired of the stuffy atmosphere of Japanese companies and seek other opportunities? In another vein, are they here for the money or the challenge?

If you can reach beyond the ''facts'' to the motivation, you may be able to recruit some promising personnel. They will still not be the kind that Japanese companies feel comfortable with. But they will be more at home with a *gaishi* and could make a useful contribution, more useful than your standard Japanese *sarariman*.

Your choice is further complicated by the tendency of some Japanese seeking employment with foreign companies to adopt a ''foreign'' manner. They shake hands vigorously, use first names and speak more loudly. They may also express admiration of your native country, recount their visits there, and praise your efforts at whatever you happen to be doing. The young ladies also have ways of ingratiating themselves. These people are certainly easier to get along with, at least for you. But, how do they relate to other Japanese, more conservative ones who will form the bulk of your staff?

Picking the right personnel is one of the toughest challenges you will face. And the cards are clearly stacked against you. But, even if you cannot get the very best team in the eyes of the Japanese, you can assemble one that is better than most foreign companies. And, if you choose wisely, it will serve you well in competing with Japanese rivals, too.

Japanizing the Staff

Strangely enough, despite the exceptional difficulty in finding staff, foreign managers are constantly under pressure to Japanize the staff entirely. This means to replace the expatriates gradually with Japanese counterparts until very few are left, perhaps only the general manager or a shadow chairman. Even they, it is argued, should eventually be replaced by locals. With an entirely Japanese staff, you should do better.

No matter how often I hear this argument, and I hear it

more and more, I find it suspect for various reasons. The first is who it eminates from. Although mouthed by docile foreigners, this concept clearly comes from the Japanese personnel of *gaishi* who want to increase their own possibilities of promotion, not only upward but to the very top. Many also feel more comfortable working under fellow Japanese, not in the least because life would be less complicated. Their views are echoed by Japanese companies which would love to see the *gaijin* go home and leave control to Japanese staff they sense is inferior to their own.

Other objections are more concrete. If it is hard to find a middle-manager, or even a decent secretary, how much more difficult must it be to find an appropriate chief executive officer? He must have a knowledge of the field and the products, he must be able to manage a staff which has been put together from various sources rather than one he grew out of, and he must liaise effectively with the head office. No matter how good he may be at the first two, he will probably have trouble with the third task.

More than that, he may find it difficult to balance the interests of the local staff and the overseas directors. Given the intimacy of Japanese offices, the way employees constantly interact and tighten relations, he is more likely to become the spokesman of the Japanese operation than its master, which is what the head office wants. While this would please the Japanese staff, no company is established for that purpose and this could cause friction which would be negative in the longer term.

The foreign executive will certainly relate less well to the local staff, but he will communicate better with the head office and will perhaps have enough clout there to impose his will when it really matters. He is also more likely to regard the success of the operation, as opposed to the comfort of the staff, as uppermost. He may push them harder. In doing so, he may also ensure the company's success and their continued employment. He should, of course, be sympathetic and understanding. But this should not get in the way of making hard decisions.

Yet more important, whether he is right or wrong in any specific instance, the *gaijin* executive is essential to provide alternatives. Group think is the curse of every Japanese organization and a foreigner, whatever his views, helps break the mold and seek original, non-Japanese solutions. This is a vital contribution to a staff which, as we saw, must do things differently to make up for other lacks.

Given the crucial role of top management, Jackson N. Huddleston, Jr. feels that the key post of general manager should go to a foreigner, someone who comes from the company rather than an outside hire and has the backing of the head office. He would be "both the head-office man in Japan and the Japan man in head office." Still, no matter how good he may be, a *gaijin* general manager/president is an alien. There are some things a Japanese can do better. He therefore suggests the possibility of having a Japanese chairman. "This individual would be responsible for enhancing external government, customer, supplier, and university relationships."[5]

The ultimate concern is one that applies to the whole Japanese staff, from a possible CEO down to the lowest level. No matter how hard it is to recruit staff, it is yet harder to discard staff.[6] Even if someone does not work out, indeed, proves to be incompetent, or you must retrench for economic reasons, it will be difficult to fire a person hired on the (tacit) assumption of lifetime employment. Regular employees often form unions and, even if they don't, will be supported by the labor authorities. It may be a long, painful and costly process to get rid of unwanted personnel, one only less daunting than keeping them.

This should not be seen as an objection to Japanization. The principle is excellent and efforts should be made in this direction as soon as possible. But it is necessary to proceed cautiously and be aware of the pitfalls that do exist. You can learn more about that by chatting with experienced Japan hands at the foreign chamber or club. The practicalities are described in two interesting books by Thomas Nevins. So, even while recruiting, you must consider how to handle dismissals if you don't want to be stuck with lifetime employees you would rather not have.

NOTES

1. For interesting comments on the problem of seeking and selecting personnel, from a practical viewpoint, see Kang, op. cit., pp. 117–82, Huddleston, op. cit., pp. 19–69, and Maurer, op. cit., pp. 65–83.
2. For pointers on recruitment techniques, see Thomas J. Nevins, *Labor Pains and the Gaijin Boss* and *Taking Charge in Japan*.
3. Maurer, op. cit., p. 79.
4. Nevins, "Six Strategic Tools for Business Success in Japan," *Journal of the ACCJ*, March 1989, p. 26.
5. Huddleston, op. cit., p. 17. For frank comments on whether to hire expatriates or Japanese for top posts, see also pp. 8–17.
6. On the difficulties of dismissals, see Nevins, *Taking Charge in Japan*.

7
Distribution

Distribution seems to be a headache everywhere, but rarely more so than in Japan, at least among the more liberal economies. It is certainly much harder than selling goods in the United States, an uncommonly open and transparent market, and even more difficult than operating in Europe or parts of East Asia. Indeed, the complexities have often appeared so formidable that distribution was branded a nontariff barrier.[1]

The most obvious problem, and one that is painfully evident even to the Japanese, is that the distribution system is oversized. In Japan, there are almost twice as many retailers per 1,000 persons as in the United States. There are also three times as many wholesalers per retailer. The differentials are not as extreme for Europe or elsewhere, although they remain substantial. Not only are there many distributors, you may have to pass through several layers before reaching the consumer.

This makes the system unwieldy. It also makes it costly. One reason is that goods are carried in small amounts and delivered on short deadlines, precluding many economies of scale or savings on transportation. They also have to be stored in strategically placed warehouses, another unwanted expense. And they can be readily returned by the retailers. To this must be added the margin imposed for these services by each of the many agents goods pass through. No wonder prices are so high!

These are problems faced by all producers, foreign and domestic. But this is a system that places a premium on long-standing relations. Once in the market, it is easier to hang on and harder to be ejected. Newcomers, on the other hand, often have to wait for an opening and then pay dearly for the privilege of being carried, in terms of commissions, rebates, etc. So, while not actually biased against foreigners, it does discriminate against newcomers which most foreigners tend to be.

It is also manipulated by insiders. This is often attributed to the supposed affection for long-standing relations and respect for the long-time important customer (*otokuisan*). You know, "my father sold his father's goods, now I sell his goods. We are used to doing business together." More likely reasons are that the supplier has some control over the distributor, either through shareholding, placing employees on the staff, financing, etc. In the worst case, they are part of the same *keiretsu* or the outlets are actually controlled by the manufacturer.

Can the distribution system be regarded as a nontariff barrier and in some way "unfair?" The Japanese say, no. And it is hard to argue that the complexity, cost or even lack of accessibility to newcomers was designed to block foreigners, although this often happens in practice. But the inter-company links are clearly discriminatory and sometimes even illegal under Japan's own legislation.

Be that as it may, you cannot possibly sell in Japan without getting into the distribution network no matter how difficult or impenetrable it may be—or appear. You have to find your own entry point, expand it, improve the terms and conditions, and become more of an insider. As intimated, while doing so you may find some of the difficulties are not as bad as they appeared at first sight. And you should be pleased to discover that reforms and improvements are facilitating your task.

Wholesale and Retail Channels

Normally, you or your agent will have to enter through the multitude of wholesalers (*tonya*). There are almost half-a-million of them, differentiated by level (primary, secondary, tertiary), size (from hundreds of employees to a handful), geographic coverage (specific regions) and product (foodstuffs, machinery, garments, etc.). In your own line, there may be literally hundreds to choose from and you may feel at a loss.[2]

Still, the large number and broad choice have certain advantages and are preferable to the opposite. That is because amongst them you can probably find one or more that suit your purpose and are not already tied to your competitors to the extent that you cannot use them. Obviously, you would tend toward wholesalers specialized in your sector. The fact that few are truly national does not hurt; after all, you cannot afford national coverage at the outset anyway. Rather, you can try one of the major cities, expand to others, and only gradually push toward the outer prefectures.

If you are a very small company, with only one or two products to market, then you may do well enough with just one wholesaler. If not, you will have to piece together a patchwork of wholesalers to get the coverage you want. In so doing, you must be careful to avoid overlap and thus competition among them. And you will have to deal with primary wholesalers, leaving them to handle the secondary and tertiary wholesalers. If you do have several, quite different products, you may have to do this a second and third time.

Some marketing specialists say the best idea is to use fewer wholesalers so that your business accounts for a larger share of their turnover. They would therefore be more beholden to you and do a better job. On the other hand, argue other specialists, such wholesalers would not be under as much pressure to perform. It would therefore be preferable to spread your business and monitor the results so you know which are best. But, returning to the first specialists, you should not spread it so thin that you have no clout. Once again, the best solution lies somewhere in the middle.

Leaving the wholesalers to deal with the retailers, while limiting your control of the operation, reduces your commitment in time, manpower and funds. For this side of the business is also not as simple as back home. As noted, goods must be supplied to numerous retailers, about a million of those. They range from fairly large (but not of American dimensions) to tiny ''mom-and-pop'' stores.

These retailers, even the most insignificant, make considerable demands. Goods must be delivered in small quantities since they lack space. Deliveries must be frequent, especially for fresh produce. Quality must be impeccable. And goods can be returned at any time with no questions asked. This can be due to defects or simply that they did not move. In addition, wholesalers are expected to pitch in and sell. They have to provide promotional staff to the retailers, etc. Finally, they sometimes finance the retailers by leaving long payment times or providing special rebates for being a good customer.

Of course, you could try to get rid of the middleman because he is costly and interrupts the flow of information from the customer. But that would not be recommended aside from exceptional cases. You will be stuck with much of the cost and hassle. According to Huddleston, ''what makes products so expensive is the marketing, sales, and service costs. But to circumvent the many intermediate costs might be even more expensive.''[3] Also, although there is some change, the old saying still holds: ''you can't fight the *tonya*.'' You probably need them much more than they need you.

Still, it is helpful to remember that the retailers are also diversified and some now offer interesting possibilities. Working your way up, there are specialty and convenience stores, most of them quite small and with little interest in or ability to sell foreign goods. Then come the general merchandise stores and superstores (*supa*), an upgraded supermarket of sorts. They do have some interest and handle some imports. On the top, with regard to size and also price, are the department stores (*depato*). These latter sell an increasing amount of imported or otherwise foreign goods. Indeed, they have become a major outlet for trendy, upmarket fashions, cosmetics, goods suitable for gift-giving, and speciality foods.

These department stores, however, are not strictly comparable to most Western ones. While they buy, stock and sell many products on their own, they also lease areas or rooms in which the leasee sells its own goods with its own personnel. This is done in return for rent and/or a commission on sales. This so-called ''shop-in-the-shop'' has become the preferred solution for many *gaishi,* especially those in the sectors mentioned above. You will encounter all the famous brand names there, from Georges Armani to Calvin Klein.

Capitalizing on Change

The older distribution channels have long served as points of entry for foreign products. Unfortunately, as noted, they only absorbed relatively limited amounts. Also, due to costs, they tended to carry more expensive, luxurious goods, where higher margins are possible. Indeed, there was a whole category of *hakuraihin* or Western imports with overtones of ''luxuries.'' Now, however, the system is opening up more widely and offering more opportunities for other types of merchandise.[4]

In wholesaling, one interesting phenomenon is the cash-and-carry wholesaler, where local retailers with fewer demands for service and ready cash simply buy what they want. This keeps costs down for the wholesaler, retailers and also imported goods. They may be handled in large enough quantities to justify entry. In retailing, there are more "independent" distributors, even of electronics, cameras and other articles that are usually sold through captive outlets. They, too, have some room for imported goods.

Increasingly, price is becoming a significant consideration for Japanese consumers. Thus, some of the general merchandise, speciality and convenience stores, although not yet the department stores, are stocking up on cheaper goods from nearby countries. This is particularly true for textiles, garments, furniture, household appliances, etc. from "newly industrializing countries." In fact, a chain of NIC Stores opened a while back. While less interested in cheap goods per se, the department stores are establishing buying offices abroad so that whatever they do get is cheaper.

Other trends in retailing are even more promising. One is the rapid growth in the number of chain stores. These stores are supplied by central buying agencies which can more readily seek out imported goods which are introduced to broaden their range and enhance their image. Of particular interest are members of large groups, like Seibu and Tokyu, which have whole retailing empires, and which can import in a big way. (See page 115.) To compete, smaller retailers have been forming joint purchasing operations.

If your product is in the middle-to-low range, and price competitive, these can be useful entry points. They are also relatively accessible. You can make contact with the head office, probably in Tokyo. In many cases, you can even initiate relations back home through the various purchasing offices or Japanese stores located in your own country. While *you* cannot get around the middleman, such big retailers can. Do not count on splitting the difference, though, you won't get a much better price. But you will avoid many complications.

Equally intriguing is the development of certain channels which were once regarded as closed to foreigners or terribly un-Japanese but have since become worthwhile alternatives.

Tokyu Retailing & Distribution Group

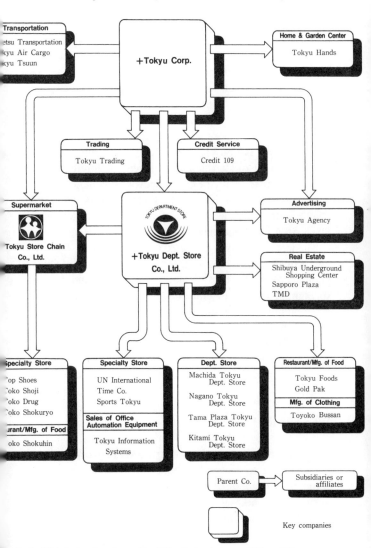

Transportation
etsu Transportation
kyu Air Cargo
kyu Tsuun

+Tokyu Corp.

Home & Garden Center
Tokyu Hands

Trading
Tokyu Trading

Credit Service
Credit 109

Supermarket
Tokyu Store Chain Co., Ltd.

+Tokyu Dept. Store Co., Ltd.

Advertising
Tokyu Agency

Real Estate
Shibuya Underground Shopping Center
Sapporo Plaza
TMD

Specialty Store
op Shoes
oko Shoji
oko Drug
oko Shokuryo

urant/Mfg. of Food
oko Shokuhin

Specialty Store
UN International
Time Co.
Sports Tokyu

Sales of Office Automation Equipment
Tokyu Information Systems

Dept. Store
Machida Tokyu Dept. Store
Nagano Tokyu Dept. Store
Tama Plaza Tokyu Dept. Store
Kitami Tokyu Dept. Store

Restaurant/Mfg. of Food
Tokyu Foods
Gold Pak

Mfg. of Clothing
Toyoko Bussan

Parent Co. → Subsidiaries or affiliates

Key companies

it: Dodwell Marketing Consultants, *Retail Distribution in Japan,* 1988, p. 217.

There is a tremendous amount of door-to-door selling in Japan. It is labor-intensive, it is costly, it is whatever you like. But, if you cannot sell through wholesalers or retailers controlled by your Japanese rivals, at least you can try this route. It has worked quite nicely for Amway, Max Factor and Elektrolux. *Gaishi* also pioneered more informal networks of part-time sales personnel, usually women, following the ''party'' route. This has been done by Amco, Shaklee and Tupperware.

Direct marketing has also been used by foreign companies, with considerably more success than initially expected. One good example is Franklin Mint. Even more encouraging are efforts at mail order sales with dozens of foreign catalogs joining the lists. Still, in this endeavor, it is helpful to have a Japanese partner. Thus, Sears has worked with Seibu, Quelle with Matsuzakaya, and Seven-Eleven is compiling a Shop America home catalog.[5]

The last alternative, just to go out and buy land, build your own store and hire your own staff, was traditionally the least popular. With the cost of land, construction and personnel so high, it is easy to understand why. But there were also psychological inhibitions. They have since dissipated. Now many automakers, especially upmarket ones, have their own dealerships rather than using agents. And the biggest incursions are coming. Both Toys 'R' Us and Blockbuster Video intend to open hundreds of stores the length and breadth of Japan.

Who Should Distribute?

Given the complexity of the distribution network, the initial reaction was to leave distribution to a Japanese agent. It could be a *sogo shosha,* a specialized trader, a sole import agent or a wholesaler. This remains by far the preferred path. Still, as has been pointed out repeatedly, there can be disadvantages.

For a start, leaving distribution to your associate allows it to decide on many crucial points, from display and presentation to sales price. It also leaves you with much less feedback. You do not really know how well sales are going, what aspects of the product are liked or disliked by retailers or customers, what you could do to boost sales. You will never even begin building a long-term relationship with those who sell your goods nor will you learn much about changing fads and fashions.

Aside from that, as previously noted, it is hard to determine just how aggressively your agent is promoting you. You do not know whether it has relations with another company that offers similar products, to which it gives preference.[6] You will not have the slightest warning if it asks some related company to design and manufacture similar products, and then dumps you. Should it do so, you will have no contacts with the retailers which had been handling your goods and have to start from scratch with another distribution network.

These drawbacks will probably lead you to ask somewhere alone the line: should we let others distribute for us or should we distribute on our own?

There is no abstract answer to that question. It depends on many things. One is how well your agent has been doing. Maybe there is no cause for complaint. Even if it does not give complete satisfaction, it is far from certain that you can do any better. The Japanese distribution system is inherently complex and costly, and you cannot get around that. Worse, it is riddled with special links and personal relationships that would be very hard to alter. If you go about things the wrong way, you may find that no wholesaler or distributor will want to deal with you.

However, the best way of answering the question is not with a flat ''yes'' or ''no.'' There are many alternatives and a whole gradation of responses. Each will take you a step further in the direction of doing your own thing and you can stop when you feel a comfortable point has been reached.

For example, while sticking to your old distributor, you can add a presence in Japan. You can staff an office which will follow up the sales effort and also contribute to it. You can have detailmen and women who go out to the retailers, get to know them, find out how they like each product and determine what you can do to help sell it. If this is coordinated in advance with the wholesaler, it should not mind and might actually be pleased with the backup.

You can certainly do more advertising and promotion of a general nature. This could consist of an ad campaign or increased availability of point-of-sale material. It could also go as far as sending your staff off to the retailer, to sell your products. After all, no one knows your products better than your own staff nor should be more motivated to sell. While this is not done often in the West, it is a common practice in Japan and many retailers come to expect it.

Given the limited scope of most wholesalers, you may have to add to those you originally chose as you expand sales or move into new regions. It is not easy to determine which ones to pick from afar. Local personnel could do a much better job of evaluating the possibilities and arranging for the right distributors. They could coordinate the efforts of the various wholesalers and avoid possible overlap or competition. They could also more readily determine which ones are doing the best job.

If, after carefully weighing the pros and cons, you do decide that distribution is too important to be left to others, you would now be in a much better position to take charge. If, the other possible scenario, your erstwhile partner failed to treat you properly or simply dropped you, you would find it easier to snap back. Or, and this is the third alternative, you may want to stick to your older distributors with your older products and try to create your own network for new ones.[7]

Whatever the case, since you will have to live with Japanese distributors and wholesalers, you should try to deal with them as effectively as possible. P. Reed Maurer, who was earlier responsible for the Japan operations of Eli Lilly and Merck, learned a lot about that. Here are some of his positive suggestions.

"Approach wholesalers fully recognizing that they are the single channel to customers. You need them more than they need you. They are able to 'push' products through the system.

Concentrate on a select group of wholesalers with wide geographic distribution capabilities.

Devote resources to establishing a 'wet' relationship with wholesaler salesmen. They know your customer.

Train wholesaler salesmen with the same intensity you train your own representatives."[8]

Profit Versus Market Share

Before concluding, it is necessary to address one crucial item which, for some odd reason, is usually overlooked even in books on doing business in Japan. Yet, it is the most important thing for any foreign businessman—profit. Many authors seem to assume that the honor of just selling in Japan, of carrying your company's brand to the natives and raising your country's flag on this inhospitable shore should be reward enough. Alas, as we know, it is impossible to remain in business very long without profits. And, if you do not earn a suitable return, the head office will quickly recall you.

Yet, making a profit in Japan is not easy. Worse, unlike most other markets where profit maximization is regarded as a normal purpose of business, in Japan there is a competing goal, namely increasing market share. This superordinate goal creates difficulties not only for Americans or Europeans, it fazes most Asians as well. You must therefore come to terms with the alternatives and decide which one you want to give higher priority.

The case for profits is fairly straightforward. Your company is making an investment, one of many possible investments, and it wants to earn a reasonable return. By now, it is generally conceded that Japan is a tougher market, it takes longer to turn a profit, and there are certain non-monetary advantages to being there. Still, the head office would find it unacceptable to lower expectations dramatically. The case for market share is that, even if you earn less on each unit, you can conceivably earn more by selling a large number of units. That is also comprehensible to the head office. Unfortunately, in practice, this usually results in less impressive earnings, at least in earlier stages.

The problem is that while you are striving for profit you are competing with Japanese companies that are avidly seeking market share. This means that each time they lower their margin to boost sales, you must do the same. Then, to keep up, they lower their margin again, and you are forced to tag along. This will continue until some company has clearly gained an edge and quite possibly others have been driven under.

So, the most telling argument of fans of market share is that if you lose too much you will disappear from the market and have no profit. It might be added, since this does not occur to them, if they cut margins too far there will be no profit, and disappearance will also be the natural outcome. The key to survival, alongside quality, delivery, etc. is thus financing. It is unlikely that your company will have as deep pockets as theirs and, even if it does, being foreign and more intent on profit, it is unlikely to dig as deep.

This means that the best approach is to strike some compromise between the competing goals. You can attempt to expand market share as long as it only involves tolerable reductions in margins but you would avoid what the Japanese call *kato kyoso* or "excessive competition." This may, however, force you to adapt your marketing policy. If you want to maintain margins, you may have to look for a niche and, at least initially, restrict yourself to rather special products. If you want to sell standard products, which appeal to the broad public, it is hard to avoid Japanese-style competition.

This is a decision which must be made consciously. Obviously, the specific products will make a difference. Some by their very nature are geared more to the broad consumer market and are sufficiently undifferentiated that it would be hard to demand a price premium. Others, especially luxury goods, are designed to be sold in smaller quantities. Indeed, with exclusivity the selling point, there is no sense in fighting for market share. Most products fall in between these extremes. Yet, for every product, no matter how ordinary or exclusive, it is possible to combine both approaches, lowering margins a bit to sell more, raising them to boost profit. It is necessary to find the right mix.

Often, the choice will not be entirely yours to make. If you are working through an importer or agent, it is quite likely that the goal will be to create a niche which benefits from the uniqueness or "foreignness" of your product. In fact, it may well be absorbed in the category of *hakuraihin*. This makes it feasible to raise prices and achieve quite extraordinary margins. This step may be taken by your agent, especially if it has exclusive rights, with rather little concern for your views. The big question then is who rakes in the profits.

On the other hand, if you are part of a joint venture, it is likely that your partner will be aiming at the broader market. Indeed, you probably chose it because it has considerable marketing clout and can move large quantities of product. It would then want to sell at the lowest possible price to gain a foothold and later expand sales. This urge for expansion may not be a passing phase, it may continue favoring market share over profit in the long run. This could result in smaller profits than a more moderate push would generate.

Only if you run a wholly owned operation can you decide on your own what the mix between profit and market share should be. That is one more reason to think of this particular solution despite the relative simplicity of going through an importer or setting up a joint venture.

NOTES

1. For further background on distribution and marketing, see Erich Batzer and Helmut Laumer, *Marketing Strategies and Distribution Channels for Foreign Companies in Japan,* and Czinkota and Woronoff, op. cit. For practical details, see Dodwell, *Industrial Goods Distribution in Japan* and *Retail Distribution in Japan,* and appropriate JETRO publications.
2. For information on wholesalers and retailers, see Dodwell, *Retail Distribution in Japan,* and JETRO's *Japan Trade Directory.*
3. Huddleston, op. cit., p. 180.
4. On changes in the distribution sector, see Czinkota and Woronoff, op. cit., pp. 109–27.
5. For more on direct marketing, see Dodwell, *Direct Marketing in Japan.*
6. To find the links of some major distributors, see Dodwell, *Industrial Groupings in Japan.* For information on who sells to whom, see Dodwell, *Retail Distribution in Japan.* On the specific situation in two important sectors, see Dodwell, *Key Players in the Japanese Electronics Industry* and *The Structure of the Japanese Auto Part Industry.*
7. For an analysis of how several foreign companies tackled their marketing problems, see Huddleston, op. cit., pp. 168–95.
8. Maurer, op. cit., pp. 138–9.

8

Keys To Success

Every book on doing business in Japan has a section on what it takes to succeed. This is mine. It includes many of the standard clichés with regard to adapting to the market, quality, service, and delivery. But it adds some items most other writers tend to neglect. It is hard to grasp why. After all, price is a crucial element anywhere, including Japan.[1] And, in Japan, nothing is quite as precious as connections.

Naturally, this section is full of dos and don'ts. It seems there is no end to the demands placed on foreign businessmen. However, remember that local businessmen are also expected to comply and, in a fiercely competitive situation, it would be unwise not to do at least as well, although I do not insist that *gaijin* must invariably perform better than the Japanese to succeed. There is plenty of room in the market for good, acceptable and even fair-to-middling companies along with the superior ones.

Although the demands appear stringent, many of them are not specific to Japan. If anything, they should be part of every company's internal requirements. It would be unwise to let up on quality, service or delivery anywhere, whether in other foreign markets or at home. It is just that expectations are somewhat higher in Japan. If you cannot meet these expectations, or at least make a serious effort to be as good as the rest, perhaps you should write off the Japanese market now and close the book on this page.

Adaptation

It is already rather hackneyed to remind foreign businessmen that Japan is a different place and thus one must adapt products and practices to it. There have been more than enough revelations of bloopers in this respect. For example, Sears trying to sell huge refrigerators to folks with tiny apartments, American automakers refusing to provide right-hand drive or computer makers failing to include *kanji* capabilities. There are plenty more and you will read about them in the press. Let us hope that they do not do an article on you one day.

There are many things to take into consideration. One is obviously the physical size of the average Japanese, considerably smaller than Americans although not that far off from some Europeans and most Asians. There is also the physical size of their living accomodations, not quite a ''rabbit hutch'' but hardly spacious enough for standard Western household appliances and consumer durables. To this must be added that, since refrigerators are small, processed foods should also come in smaller portions.

Japanese also have different tastes. There are some colors they like more or less than others. There are certain fabrics they fancy more or less. There is also the element of texture, usually neglected in foodstuffs or clothing elsewhere but often decisive for Japanese shoppers. They are also particularly sensitive to odors, another factor frequently overlooked abroad. Aside from that, remember that the voltage may differ and Japan uses centimeters, not inches. Many more items could be added to the list but should be carefully sought out in connection with your own products.

Another more general point is that the Japanese lavish more energy on packaging than most. That is particularly important since so many items are bought as gifts. This can involve an abundant, even exaggerated use of boxes, paper, ribbons, etc. For some articles, like fruit or candies, each individual unit must be suitably packed and then the whole thing wrapped up to please the purchaser.

Less often mentioned, but no less significant, goods must sometimes be distributed through different channels. Some almost have to pass through the *sogo shosha* first. Others may be sold in department stores, but not by the store itself, you have to run the operation in leased space. With so many captive outlets for household appliances, consumer electronics, cosmetics, watches, etc., you may have to create your own channels. Whatever is categorized as *hakuraihin* or foreign "luxuries" will get very special treatment, often through a sole agent. Moreover, like it or not, your goods are likely to pass through more hands before reaching the end-user.

Advertising, as you have doubtlessly heard by now, is quite different on the whole. There is much more attention to mood, trying to convey the intrinsic value of the product often with scarcely any mention thereof. Indeed, in some commercials, you don't even see the product. There is scant reference to its function or how it fulfills it. And talk of price—let alone that it is cheaper than the competitor's—is still regarded as off bounds.

There is no need to dwell on this. Just read any article on advertising in Japan and it will tell you, first, that things are different and, secondly, that you had better comply. Should you be so imperious as to insist that what you do back home might work here and the agency will deliver a long lecture on why it cannot work in Japan. In most cases, the Japanese (and assimilated foreign) agencies are right. But not always. And things are changing. So ask for slightly more objective reasons and perhaps try your idea out in a small way somewhere along the line. It may be different; but then, so are you and your product.

There are several other variations on the theme of adapting. For example, you should adapt your payment conditions to local circumstances. Your wholesalers, and their retailers, would like to have as long to pay you as to pay Japanese suppliers. If, on the other hand, you are the purchaser and you are procuring Japanese goods, you should demand standard conditions for that. Since delays in payment may be longer than you are accustomed to, you should probably keep more money in the bank while you are waiting.

Another practice, perhaps even less palatable but unavoidable, is that retailers have the right to return not only goods they regard as defective but those that do not sell. According to Michael Czinkota, a specialist in marketing, returns run two to five times as high as in the United States. Maybe you don't have to accept such extensive return privileges back home. In Japan, you would be wise not to complain and comply with their wishes . . . if you want to hold on to your distribution network and clientele. You would be even wiser not to introduce the wrong goods or allow defects to begin with.

Still, given the widespread criticism of *gaishi* for not adapting, it should be noted that some have done rather well at it. Most cosmetics companies tailored products specifically for Japanese tastes, Max Factor already having done that for over half its line. Apple, whose computers were initially user-unfriendly, added *kanji* capabilities, as have most other vendors. Ore-Ida made smaller portions and packages of frozen potatoes because Japanese have smaller appetites and freezers. Coca-Cola actually developed products solely for Japan, including a coffee drink and a health drink. McDonald's makes the same sort of hamburgers, but it sells them in urban centers more than the suburbs.[2]

Quality

You would really have to be living in a cave not to know by now that the Japanese are fanatic about quality. This starts with the manufacturers, who hone their production techniques and quality control to come up with articles having the least defects possible, and then improve on that the next time around. If this is what your competitors are doing, then you had better do the same thing. You had better raise your quality standards to the Japanese level and keep going, because they will continue rising.[3]

This is not just to satisfy what sometimes appears to be an exaggerated urge for perfection. If you do not keep up, you will lose your clientele. This applies especially to makers of parts and components or equipment bought by Japanese manufacturers. They can be terribly exacting with suppliers. You must also please the ordinary consumer, who is more demanding than most Americans, French or whatever. Japanese consumers will not buy visibly defective products. And they will return those which subsequently turn out to be defective (or simply don't work). The retailer will then pass these rejects on to the wholesaler who will present them to you.

By the way, it is not only a question of defects which affect the product's use or functioning. The product may work well enough. But it will still not appeal to those who expect each part to be just right. And many consumers are turned off by cosmetic defects which would pass elsewhere, such as uneven painting, scratches or other blemishes. They may be symptomatic, or so it is reasoned, of deeper, hidden failings.

Obviously, no matter what you do, defects will continue to exist even in the most meticulous operations. But keeping them down, and reducing the number per thousand (or million) will certainly impress Japanese clients. Moreover, keeping them closer to the mean will consolidate relations. One bad lot can spoil the positive impression of a dozen good ones. It demonstrates a lack of regularity that could have unpleasant consequences.

Not as often mentioned, but perfectly self-evident, is that Japan has its own standards. Japan Industrial Standards are very strict, and this can be a first hurdle for foreign makers.[4]

They may also be somewhat idiosyncratic. Unlike many others, which simply require that basic parameters be met, they may specify size, position of parts, techniques used and so on. This can go to the point that they are disguised nontariff barriers. Fair or not, logical or not, they must be complied with.

Delivery

The Japanese are also exceedingly strict on delivery. You must get the goods to them on time, exactly at the time indicated. There is no excuse for anything else. Once again, this is already part of the structure. Most companies work on the basis of the just-in-time system and retailers insist on getting products promptly, which means that wholesalers do the same with even greater insistence.

They are not merely being sticklers. There are reasons why the Japanese have to tighten up deadlines. The main cause is the lack of space. Manufacturers simply do not have the space to carry large inventories or parts so they must be delivered to the assembly line as needed. Most retailers have very small stores and even the larger ones have little storage room. They have to replace their inventory almost as the products are sold. Admittedly, they have become overly demanding of late, expecting ever smaller shipments at ever closer deadlines. But there is nothing you can do about it.

Thus, if you want to become a regular supplier to a Japanese manufacturer or maintain good relations with the various distributors, you must adjust to this situation. Since you cannot possibly produce at the same pace as they order goods, you will need more storage space despite the high cost. You will want to be very certain that deliveries from back home arrive on time and, if necessary, air freight goods. You may even consider whether, to avoid any threat of delays, you do not want to produce locally.

Failing to provide prompt and regular delivery could be disastrous, as serious as failing to maintain quality. The Japanese consumer, retailer, wholesaler and/or manufacturer would regard you as an unreliable partner. The next step would normally be to seek a Japanese one which could meet the requirements.

Service

When business consultants are not lecturing you on quality, quality, quality, they are probably clucking: service, service, service. That is another indispensable requirement for doing business in Japan, a country with more such requirements than most. But service sometimes appears even less comprehensible—and attainable—a goal than quality.[5]

Of course, you should supply goods without defects, blemishes, etc. And that happens to be the first aspect of good service for a foreign firm. You should also guarantee prompt and regular delivery. That is a second aspect. But you have to go much further.

As noted, Japanese consumers place more stress on packaging than elsewhere. In fact, they sometimes care more about how a gift is wrapped than what it's worth. Well, this love of appearances spreads to the outlets themselves. The Japanese love to shop in pleasant surroundings, in an environment which leads them to feel that they are indeed very special beings. This involves more luxuriously appointed premises than would be necessary elsewhere. The address should be right, in the correct shopping district for the clientele targeted. Don't skimp on this to save money on rent!

They also enjoy viewing plenty of sales personnel. Customers do not like to wait to be served. Most department stores, and even more so the boutiques, have excess staff hanging around just in case someone should walk in. Most of the time, however, they stand about doing nothing. Repeat.

They stand, not sit. And they remain attentive, not chatting, gossiping or reading a magazine, but ready to receive the customer should one appear. Another seemingly unnecessary, or at least doubtful, expense.

This personnel, by the way, is not just anybody. Salesgirls are very carefully chosen to look pleasant but not too attractive, to wear the right clothing (often the company uniform), to appear demure at all times and to bow low in the appropriate fashion to each and every customer. They bow low physically on occasion. Otherwise this demeanor is expressed by using the politest language. The men are similarly selected and schooled, if not quite as subservient. This implies recruiting higher class personnel than elsewhere, with a better education and social graces than elsewhere, and also more expensive than elsewhere.

And don't think *you* will get off any easier. You may be an executive in a major foreign manufacturer, but if you sell products to the Japanese, as noted, you are at least a rung further down the social ladder than the companies you sell to, whether manufacturers or distributors. You are two rungs beneath the final consumer. If there are complaints, from the customer or consumer, you can expect to be called in to explain. You had better adopt the right demeanor, strike the appropriate posture, and apologize in suitably soothing terms. Don't bother with rational explanations of what happened and how it won't be repeated. Apologize for all you are worth!!!

By now you must have noticed a repeated refrain. Service costs. It costs in packaging, rent and decoration. It costs in wages. Above all, it costs in time. How can you possibly provide all this extra service and make any money? Well, I will let you in on a secret that most other authors do not seem privy to. You have to charge for it! Calculate all the additional costs and put them in your price. The Japanese do it. Why shouldn't you?

Price

While they are full of advice on quality, delivery and service,
most books on doing business in Japan don't bother with the
issue of price. Perhaps that is insufficiently academic for the
professors. But for businessmen it is crucial (sorry to use that
word again). With costs likely to be higher than expected,
prices must be set appropriately so you get something for
your effort.

The question of pricing is rather complex for foreign companies in Japan because most tend to be at the top or the
bottom end. You have the brand name producers, often selling
luxury items in special shops or boutiques. Even for more
standard products, like clothing or automobiles, it is the upmarket products which have done best, whether Dior or
BMW. Then come the food specialities, wine from France,
chocolate from Switzerland, cheese from Holland. Even the
fast food joints, which would be regarded as quite ordinary
back home, have a deeper appeal. They all participate in the
category of *hakuraihin*.

Well, for foreign imported goods at the top end, normal
pricing does not apply. You do not usually price at the same
level as local competitors, let alone somewhat lower, but
appreciably higher. For many of the articles are bought for
their foreignness, which means there is no direct equivalent.
Others are luxuries, and as such should command high prices.
Indeed, Japanese apparently feel more comfortable paying
more since this seems to prove their value. Marking prices
down only degrades the image.

Thus, many of the makers and their agents, often sole
agents, have done everything they could to enhance the snob
appeal of their products. They located sales points in appropriate places, and damn the rent. They laid on sales personnel,
and taught it to bow very low indeed. Meanwhile, they jacked
up the prices. The only problem, alas, was that some of the

goods seeped in through parallel imports (or outright counterfeits) and undermined the image.

Not surprisingly, with high prices, turnover was relatively low. This combination has worked for some and profits were heartening. To tell the truth, Japan has been a bonanza for many luxury goods makers. However, others were more marginal, not able to sell enough to do well. They are now thinking of lowering prices and targeting a broader market, which would also stem parallel imports somewhat. In short, they face the old dilemma of price versus market share in a more acute form than others. As Huddleston lucidly comments:

"By using high prices as a marketing mechanism to say that the product is quality, the foreign product's market potential is limited to the very top of the market, whether fountain pens, whiskey, men's suits, beer, or furniture. If a company only wants the premium end of the market, that is fine. The Japanese, though, will buy much more of quality products that are priced competitively and meet a need. If products are not priced competitively, the market will remain extremely limited and soon someone will come in and meet the market need created below this stratosphere."[6]

At the other end, you have the masses of ordinary products which are provided by both advanced and developing countries, but especially the nearby NICs. This includes textiles, garments, furniture, household appliances, small TVs and VCRs, and so on. They obviously sell more on price than anything. Indeed, given the Japanese preference for procuring goods at home, from suppliers they know and are related to, it is purely a question of price. Prices must be kept down even more than, say, in the United States to overcome the initial reluctance. However, the labor cost gap is so large by now that this is not an insurmountable hurdle.

There are also producers active in the middle range, if not quite as many. They are often parts suppliers or equipment makers which must compete with Japanese rivals that are about as good. This they can do with some of their latest, most innovative models, or by undercutting competitors. Some have done quite well. Others, less so. And they occasionally hang on more for reasons of pride than profit. However, with Japanese wages rising and the yen appreciating, even the Americans will eventually be able to sell more on price and still maintain a decent profit.

Connections

If the illustrious "experts" rarely say anything about price, they almost never mention connections. That is a dirty word and the ways of creating them are not fit material for serious books. Well, dirty or not, connections are vital in Japan. Without them, you cannot get anything done. With them, you can accomplish all sorts of things you thought were impossible. So, what should you do?

There are all sorts of connections, and all degrees thereof, so there can be no systematic approach to this task. But you can very well start by deciding that Japan is an essential market and you are in it for the long haul. You should not only say this. The Japanese have heard that song before. You should prove it by regularly upgrading your operation, Japanizing your personnel, etc. You do not have to go all the way. Still, just being around over the years makes you increasingly part of the scene.

You should also cultivate those long-standing relations they talk about. The best way is to keep providing good quality, delivery, service, etc. so that your counterparts want to do business with you. You should also help them sell your goods, say, by providing more POS material or sending your staff to work in their shops. By offering decent payments terms, perhaps slightly better than necessary, they will be in your debt a bit more.

And don't forget what is politely called "human relations." Cultivate your contacts. Make lots of visits. Visit your suppliers occasionally. Visit your clients frequently, even when it is not necessary. Bring around your CEO or whatever big shot happens to be in town. That will impress them with the seriousness of the company's interest in Japan and keep him out of the way. Try inviting key persons out for dinner and a drink, to help mellow the relationship.

Then come the gifts, at least twice a year at gift-giving season. There is no harm in tossing in some more. The gifts should not be too luxurious for the occasion, nor too skimpy. Especially not too skimpy. Japanese know down to the yen what a gift is worth, what sort of a gift they are worth, and what gifts others are giving them. In such circumstances, gifts can hardly be regarded as bribes. Nor can sumptuous dinners. They are part of the cost of doing business . . . and treated as such by the tax authorities.

The further steps are somewhat trickier. You will need a feel for this to avoid being awkward or even insulting and might best leave it to a Japanese staff member. It is precious to have support in the right places. You might therefore create a council of advisors, or some such, and invite suitable, senior, sociable Japanese to join. They are not chosen for their knowhow so much as their connections, which you hope will become yours. You might even recruit a retired bureaucrat from a ministry with which you have considerable contact.[7] Again, that is not unethical. It is done quite regularly, so much so that it is not easy to come by one.

So much for "human relations." Connections are also more palpable. There is no reason why, should your supplier or wholesaler be in dire financial straits, you should not advance him a reasonable sum. Better yet, buy a share in the company. That demonstrates just how much you respect it. It also gives you a degree of control. This could be consolidated by your joining the board and perhaps placing loyal employees on their staff.

With *keiretsu* so important and so pervasive, you should decide whether to tie up with one. This can be done through joint ventures, using a member as supplier, or turning to the core bank. If you are a good customer, it might urge other members to do business with you. Or course, you will not become an insider, but you will be less of an outsider than before.

Finally, this being the fashion, you could start creating your own little grouping. This means not doing everything by yourself, which is not the Japanese way to begin with. You can establish separate entities, either under your control or part of a joint venture, to handle your manufacturing, sales or other functions for you. These peripheral bodies would still be dependent on you, but not part of the inner circle nor entitled to the benefits that accrue to a "parent" company.

NOTES

1. Kang also places special stress on quality, cost/price, delivery and service as the vital factors which he sums up as QCDS. See Kang, op. cit., pp. 2–17.
2. More examples can be found in Robert C. Christopher, *Second to None*.
3. On Japanese concern with quality and product upgrading, see Imai, op. cit., and Tatsuno, op. cit.
4. For further information on Japanese standards, contact JETRO which can direct you to the pertinent standard-setting bodies and has translated some of the most useful standards into English.
5. Japan's passion for service is reflected in George Fields, *Gucci on the Ginza*.
6. Huddleston, op. cit., p. 195.
7. For comments on relations with the bureaucracy, see Huddleston, op. cit., pp. 94–107.

9

When In Japan,
Do As The Japanese?

There is probably no bit of advice you will hear or read more
frequently than that variation on an old theme: "when in
Japan, do as the Japanese." You will get it from official
sources, you will get it from well-meaning Japanese businessmen, you will get it even at seminars of foreign chambers
of commerce. It is mouthed, often parrot-like and without
much thought to the matter, by foreign businessmen themselves, especially those who do not practice what they preach.

On the face of it, it makes sense. After all, Japan is a very
different country from your own, the business climate in
particular is quite different, companies function in different
ways and the management system operates differently. More
broadly, the place has a different language, culture and customs. Doing things the way you did back home hardly seems
reasonable. Not only that, from everything you have heard
it has almost guaranteed failure for those foolish enough to
attempt it.

But that does not prove that you should do as the Japanese.
It only means that you should adapt to Japan, perhaps doing
some things like the Japanese but not necessarily everything.
There may be certain things that you can do better because
practices in your home country are more advanced or more
efficient. Why scrap them?

Moreover, even if you try to do like the Japanese in all respects, you will not succeed. You cannot. The simple fact of the matter is that *you are not Japanese*. You can hire as many Japanese personnel as you want, adopt as many Japanese practices as you want, and you will still not be Japanese. Your company will still have some *gaijin* on the staff. It will still have to respond to the head office abroad. It will still be selling products generated by a foreign entity. And it will still have to succeed in the way evaluated most highly there, namely by producing a good bottom line. More about this later.

The most conclusive reason for not falling into the trap of unthinkingly doing as the Japanese is that you will never be as good at it as the Japanese. You are a relative newcomer, unless you've been around for several decades (and even then you are hardly an insider). You don't have a staff you have grown but one acquired in various ways; you don't have solid links to other companies and useful connections to get business; you don't have any government backing to speak of. If you try to out-Japanese the Japanese, you are bound to fail. The Japanese know that perfectly well. Maybe that's why they want you to try.

No, if you hope to succeed in Japan, you had better accept the fact that you are a *gaishi* and determine what advantages can be derived from that status. As you will see, they are fairly extensive and certainly more than is commonly conceded. They have been the secret weapon of many foreign firms and can help your own. If anything, this foreign dimension can explain considerably more successes than can "doing as the Japanese."

But, You Are Not Japanese!

Don't be lulled into the illusion that, just because you have an office in Tokyo and your unmistakably foreign name is followed by a K.K., you are a Japanese company. You certainly are under the law. And you will be dealt with as such by the tax authorities. But, to most of your clients, suppliers and distributors, the officials you deal with, and even your own personnel, you are still pretty foreign.

Nowhere is this more evident than in the staffing of your company and the management style adopted. The average *gaishi* has a mixed staff. This can range anywhere from a band of expatriates plus assorted local secretaries and salesmen to just one foreign executive or advisor working with the Japanese. It may even reach the point where the boss is Japanese and there are no foreigners present physically. Yet, unless the company has been around an unusually long time, there will be some personnel who entered in mid-career and others who joined directly after graduation.

Until the whole staff has been recruited at entry level and trained up to the top executive, this mixed structure will persist and it will be hard to apply the supposedly "typical" management system. That is, everybody rising gradually, attaining higher ranks as much (if not more) through seniority than ability, reaching decisions from the bottom up, tackling assignments in groups, and so on. This would be true Japanization, as opposed to the much more limited and superficial Japanization of merely having only Japanese faces.

Yet, before deciding this is the goal, one should seriously consider whether it is worth the effort. The assumption must be that Japanese-style management actually is superior to any other conceivable form of management. As already pointed out, it is very efficient in the factory, but rather poor in the office, where it can be dreadfully slow and unimaginative. Moreover, once the local operation goes over to Japanese-style consensus management, it will increase the gap and friction with the head office, which operates on another basis.

Even if you can "Japanize" on the quick through the expedient of hiring more Japanese personnel, do not forget that—in the eyes of other Japanese—these will probably be "second-rate" personnel. That means they will come from lesser colleges or high schools, they will have had poorer grades there, they will accept the somewhat demeaning status of working for foreigners, and so on. That may not matter much to you. Indeed, you may find such a team not only easier to work with but more dynamic. But they will find it harder to do business with other Japanese companies which look down on them somewhat and regard them as pushy.

Anyway, to become part of the Japanese establishment, it takes more than Japanese staff. You must win acceptance from other Japanese companies. You must become a regular supplier or client, and this can take a very long time. It will also be inhibited by not belonging to one of their groups, be it a *keiretsu* or looser. If you enter a joint venture or cozy up to a bank, that may help. But you will be in one of the outer circles quite far from the center.

As for the bureaucrats, who really count as opposed to the politicians, they also take an inordinately long time to recognize the existence of foreign companies, let alone warm up to them. Thank goodness officials are no longer as adamant about keeping foreign companies down and there is less they can do to boost local ones. Still, you must avidly curry favor to obtain not superior but equal treatment.

Wanting to become an insider or semi-insider is a worthy ambition, but it will not be easy to achieve. And, as long as your head office lies abroad, you will never be quite like the others. After all, the head office provides most of the products even if you adapt them or develop some on your own. It decides how much R&D money will be spent and what gets the highest priority. It may even have specific ideas on how to market products, naturally preferring those which succeeded back home. There is a limit to how much you can impose on the head office and any flexibility in Japan will be restricted.

The most important aspect relates to profitability. You can argue as long as you want that the Japanese are more intent on market share, that market share does count for something here and that it can ultimately improve the bottom line. The head office is probably not willing to wait that long and will want more profits faster. That has implications of all sorts: not only how you price your products but also how you market them, whether you advertise or not, how much personnel you hire, how big an office you have, whether you manufacture and do R&D locally, etc.

By now you must have gotten the message. A *gaishi* is not a Japanese company by some legal formality or even by hiring Japanese. It will only be so superficially until it has been thoroughly acclimatized. And, even then, there will be residuals of foreignness. So, and this is the next message, if you are going to remain foreign, at least take advantage of your foreignness.

The Idea Edge

There is presently much criticism of Western companies for adopting a ''not-invented-here'' mentality and failing to realize the strengths of Japanese industry. That criticism is doubtlessly warranted. But it tends to cover over equally justifiable criticism of the Japanese, who have their own form of the ''not-invented-here'' syndrome. This is especially true now that they have become leaders in many sectors. This tends to blind them to the existence of other products which they do not produce, which they may not even care to produce because nobody else in Japan has bothered doing so. A recent survey showed that it is easier to launch a research project if similar work is being done by another Japanese firm than if it were being done abroad.

It is equally evident that now that the Japanese have pulled ahead in many sectors they have also become more arrogant about what to produce and how. This leads them to overlook many lesser products. Some of these are admittedly niche products, not terribly interesting for big companies but enough to satisfy smaller ones. Yet, some of these niches could expand massively and Japanese vanity will broaden the windows of opportunity for others.

The Japanese also lose through the tendency to focus on relatively few products at a time, giving each a major push. That is the essence of targeting.[1] However, targeting some products implies by definition overlooking or paying insufficient heed to others. Foreign businessmen should thus carefully examine Japan's priorities not only to see what will be tomorrow's winners but also where the Japanese may be losers since they cannot do everything at once.

It is not only specific products that are neglected, whole sectors get short shrift. Most of the targeting has been of industrial products, especially those that can be mass produced. Others, requiring more intricate handwork or produced in smaller runs, may not be as competitive. In other sectors, the Japanese are often poor competitors. Not only with regard to agriculture but also processed foods. The same applies to many services, from more sophisticated leasing or factoring to quite ordinary leisure or fast-food outlets. Regulated sectors have also tended to lag as companies could survive without developing new or improved products, as for insurance, consumer finance, fund management, etc. Finally, there are areas where imagination and creativity have distinct merits, such as software and leisure.

Just as serious as the "not-invented-here" syndrome is the "it-cannot-be-done-in-Japan" syndrome. This is extremely widespread, once again reinforced by the group think and increasing arrogance of Japanese businessmen. Any *gaijin* working in Japan will encounter it time and again. He will come up with a brilliant idea, or simply suggest that the Japan office copy what is done at home, and get the same stubborn reply. "It cannot be done in Japan. Maybe it can be done elsewhere, but it cannot be done in Japan."

Why?, he may ask. If he expects a rational answer, giving detailed explanations of what conditions prevent its success, let alone case histories where it has failed to work in Japan, he will be disappointed. The explanation is always the same. "It has never been done in Japan." It cannot succeed because it has never been done. . . .

If you run a Japanese-style office, you will have to leave it at that. But, if you have managed to influence it, to make it more flexible and open, you may be able to actually try the idea out. Don't assume it will work in Japan just because it worked abroad. It may not. On the other hand, it just may.[2]

There are countless examples of products which did work, from Band-Aids to Pampers. Of services which caught on, from temps to fast foods. Even of techniques, such as direct marketing and mail order catalogs. Just how wrong the "it-cannot-be-done-in-Japan" crowd can be was shown by Thomas Ainley, Jr. of McCann Direct. Direct marketing, now a booming sector, was supposedly impossible because the Japanese like to touch and see products, won't buy from a company they don't know, will not wait to have goods delivered, etc. Worse, Coca-Cola was initially warned it could not use vending machines because the Japanese would not drink directly from a bottle or can, this being too uncouth and unsanitary. Now you cannot go anywhere without finding vending machines . . . and Coke.[3]

Finally, and this should not be forgotten, many foreign products succeed quite simply because of their foreignness. For some, the foreignness should perhaps be toned down, especially if they are quite ordinary, run-of-the-mill articles. For others, it should be enhanced. After all, *hakuraihin* have traditionally done well. This does not have to be solely luxury items or upmarket fashion goods. The foreignness of automobiles is a selling point, as is the foreignness of foods and leisure pursuits.

One wrinkle on this, often passed over, is that the foreign business community is itself large enough nowadays for smaller foreign firms to live off it. This includes ventures providing services like translation, advertising, temporary employees, travel, business consulting, etc. While some of these firms are fairly big, such as Manpower and the advertising agencies, others are quite small, often just tiny shops.

The Management Edge

As I intimated more than once, even if you could replicate the "typical" Japanese management system, it is far from certain whether you should. It has many failings which foreigners tend to miss but are so obvious to Japanese executives that they are urgently calling for reforms. And where do they look for models? The West. They want to get away from pay and promotion by seniority and adopt criteria influenced more by ability and performance. They want to cut down on time-consuming discussions and dispersed decision-making which does generate consensus but also mutual irresponsibility where no one is responsible for blunders (just as no one is rewarded for good ideas).

Foreign companies should still try to adjust their employment structure to benefit from certain advantages of the Japanese system. Indeed, growing a staff rather than recruiting mid-career personnel should be a goal. So should some group work and bottom-up decision-making. But that should be tempered by a degree of reward for those who either work harder or perform better. In a mixed system, this is much easier.

That is how foreign companies can get an edge over local ones. They can stimulate their employees to think more openly and freely of different ways of doing things. They can encourage them to be more imaginative and creative. They can break away more readily from the "not-invented-here" and especially "it-cannot-be-done-in-Japan" syndromes.

Even when a foreign company adopts a specific Japanese technique, it can be modified to reduce any inherent inefficiency. For example, while adopting group action, it can limit the number of group members to those who are directly involved and discard those only vaguely concerned or who one does not wish to slight. Employees could more readily do the work for which they are paid if their jobs were more precisely defined. While it is useful to have decisions coming from the bottom, the process of moving to the top could be expedited, perhaps by requiring fewer approvals. And there is no reason why the boss should not occasionally reach decisions on his own after due consultation.

Foreign companies could certainly do a better job of allocating work, thereby raising the level of competence. While some of the staff should be rotated regularly, that might be a smaller share. More of the posts would be held by professionals, trained to do specialized tasks, such as design or accounting. Others would be kept in specific posts where they show talent or ability, such as sales or R&D. They would, of course, have to be rewarded as well as the generalists. This would surely make them more efficient and professional than many Japanese companies.

While there is plenty of room for improvement with regard to white-collar staff in general, the biggest gains could be in a rational use of women. Nowhere is the waste and futility more evident than locking women into frivolous and sometimes demeaning activities. This applies especially to those who are hired for decorative purposes, to be the "flowers of the office," and who may just run errands or do menial tasks despite a good education and solid ability. Encouraged by foreign managers, and perhaps resisted less by Japanese males who accept to work for a foreign company, they could certainly produce more than their counterparts in Japanese companies.

All of this would make for a much more dynamic team, one that is not bound down by tradition, where younger, keener men and women can contribute more and where older, more experienced ones would appreciate their efforts rather than see it as a slight or threat. This could be the true key to success of the *gaishi*.[4]

With regard to blue-collar workers, there is not that much room for improvement, since the Japanese are past masters at factory productivity. Indeed, the flow of ideas and techniques might be in the other direction, with the foreign company using its Japanese factories as a source of learning for its other operations. This could be a precious aid in enhancing competitiveness back home. The only thing that foreign bosses might impart is a bit more decency in treating ordinary workers and a bit less contempt in treating suppliers and subcontractors, which would not pay off in the short term but could improve long-term relations.

The Profit Edge

Some of the benefits of foreignness are quite simply related to costs. The most obvious is access to raw materials that are cheaper than in Japan and can thus not only be sold there but further processed to achieve added value. This is an advantage for resource-rich countries, whether advanced or developing. Given the costs of transport and electricity in Japan, there is little point to doing more processing there and such a move would probably only decrease their competitiveness.

More recently, many countries have developed a comparative advantage for labor. Japanese labor costs have risen rapidly, a move only compounded by the appreciation of the yen. By now, Japanese labor costs can be as much as four, five and six times that of countries in East and Southeast Asia.

Admittedly, some of them do not offer the same quality. But do not swallow the standard Japanese gripe about quality. The quality is quite high in many other Asian countries, if not quite at Japanese levels, certainly acceptable in general. And, considering the price differential, even somewhat lesser quality is usually tolerable.

While labor costs are close to Japanese levels in advanced countries, they can also profit from cheap labor elsewhere. They should not be put off by talk of inadequate quality and insistance that the best place to manufacture is Japan. Sometimes it is, for products that must be constantly adapted, delivered quickly or require exceptional quality. Others can just as well be produced offshore. That is proven by the fact that Japanese companies themselves now outsource many components and products.

Costs are one factor in the bottom line. Prices are another. Japanese managers tend to keep prices as low as possible in a competitive situation because they are seeking market share. Often, they keep prices lower than necessary when they could easily get away with somewhat higher ones. That is because they are more likely to be penalized for selling less units than earning less money. Foreign managers, who are taught to keep an eye on margins, often price somewhat higher. They therefore tend to get better profits.

Admittedly, as noted, there is a tradeoff. Higher profits may result in lower market share. Losing too much market share is dangerous, especially in Japan. So foreign managers must remind their head office that the bottom line is not everything. On the other hand, profits have certain advantages the Japanese often ignore. Fatter profits bring higher stock prices and thus lower financing costs. They provide cash to hire more personnel, do more research, launch more products, acquire other companies, and so on.

Whatever the case, *gaishi* have regularly generated bigger profits than Japanese companies. This was shown year after year by MITI's Survey on Foreign-Affiliated Enterprises.[5] Recently, the foreigners achieved an average ratio of ordinary profit to sales of over 6% against some 2.5% for the Japanese. What is even more interesting, although based largely on anecdotal evidence, is that apparently foreign companies with multiple overseas operations frequently obtained bigger profits in Japan than elsewhere.

There may be various explanations for this. One is probably that only more successful foreign enterprises managed to hold on in Japan. Another, more relevant, is that they paid much closer attention to the bottom line than their Japanese rivals. They also avoided some of the inefficiencies that plague Japanese companies. However it was done, this shows both that foreign managers must be doing something better than the Japanese and that having an operation in Japan can pay off.

NOTES

1. On Japanese targeting, what it involves and which sectors were picked, see Woronoff, *Japanese Targeting*.
2. This view is endorsed by President Ikehata of Spaulding Japan, who feels "you can't entirely ignore tradition. But don't get too hung up on customs. I'm a Japanese but I realize that to do something new you can't just say 'that's the way we've always done it.' " *Focus Japan*, March 1990, p. 8.
3. See Thomas Ainley, Jr., "Direct to the Heart," *Journal of the ACCJ*, June 1990, pp. 40–52.
4. For more ideas on how Japanese management can be outclassed, see Woronoff, *Japan's Wasted Workers*.
5. See MITI's *Gaishikei kigyo no doko* (Survey on Foreign-Affiliated Enterprises), annual.

10
What Now?

I don't know how often I have heard this old saw: Japan is a tough market, but once you're inside you've got it made. Unfortunately, it isn't quite that simple. Japan is a tough market. And you can do very nicely there in whatever terms you want, sales, market share, profits. But you've never really "got it made." You have to keep at it all the time. You just cannot lean back and relax because the competition never ceases and, if anything, seems to be intensifying.

That is why there are so many foreign companies which came, apparently succeeded for a while, and then quietly pulled back or disappeared. Some of them could not take the competition. Others decided they were satisfied with a niche, which they cultivated and exploited. Those, however, which reacted properly not only became successes in Japan. They were able to use the increased muscle and savvy to good effect on the home and third markets.

In this connection, it can be useful to think in terms of phases, as T.W. Kang suggested. After the first phase of recruiting personnel, establishing distribution channels and refining quality, service, etc., there comes an even more crucial second phase.

"The second phase—competitor catch-up—is where many Western firms fall down. As the foreign firm establishes a new product or service concept in Japan and its sales start to grow, Japanese competitors soon realize that this sales growth could mean good business for them as well. Because catch-up usually occurs with breathtaking speed, the foreign firm needs to anticipate such a threat. . . . a foreign firm must function at the same level of competitiveness the potential Japanese competitors strive for.''[1]

Facing the Competition

There are a lot of foreign companies which could be regarded as "three-year wonders." They arrived with a strikingly new product, an exceptional marketing strategy or particularly efficient production techniques. They had the best of all advantages, uniqueness. And their product swept the market, claiming a major share and driving back local competitors. The *gaishi* was extremely pleased with its success and the media publicized it widely. It supposedly proved what foreigners could do in Japan.

If you take up the story three years later, you find that the product is no longer doing so well. There are numerous clones on the market, most not quite as good but still eating into market share, some actually better. Local competitors are now producing more efficiently than before, occasionally outpacing the initiator. And they have adopted similar marketing techniques, some earlier eschewed because conventional wisdom proclaimed they could not work in Japan.

There is no end to the list of foreign products that were copied or topped by me-too models. Proctor & Gamble was the first into the market with strong detergents and disposable diapers, which were soon not only replicated but improved upon. Coca-Cola quickly encountered cola drinks no one had ever heard of and which could presumably be imbibed while eating unheard of (and sometimes unpronounceable) brands of pizza that capitalized on the success of Domino's. Obviously, no manufacturer was ever safe as the Japanese introduced upgraded versions of radios, televisions, motor-

cycles, automobiles, computers, and so on. The only con-
solation is that *gaishi* were not the only target. The Japanese
copied from one another just as actively.

No, you simply cannot rest on your laurels. And this is
truer today than before. Because this three-year wonder used
to be a five-year wonder and even a seven-year wonder shortly
after the war. It took the Japanese longer to catch on and
catch up before. Now, borrowing products and techniques,
whether from other Japanese companies or foreign ones is a
standard technique. For some of the bigger companies, like
Matsushita and Shiseido, it is almost their stock in trade. That
is how Matushita acquired the nickname ''Maneshita'' or
copy-cat.

The lesson is that, even while launching your product, you
have to think about the future . . . what will happen in the
next few years. You can be certain that your competitors will
immediately start trying to match it and, if possible, improve
on it in some way. That means you must be doing the same
thing so that when their me-too products reach the market,
you already have one that is somewhat better. And when they
come out with a second generation, you should already have
your third. And so on.

Meanwhile, in a more general manner, you must continue
refining the competitive factors mentioned before. It is essential to adapt products increasingly to Japanese consumer
preferences, making them smaller, thinner or whatever. You
have to improve quality all the time. Expedite your delivery
as well. And add whatever supplementary service can be
mustered. Price, as was noted, will be more important than
ever and that may be where you still have some edge over
your Japanese rivals.

This is costly, time-consuming and bothersome. You may
not want to be drawn into an endless race. Yet, as long as
your Japanese competitors continue upgrading their operations, you have to do the same. The payoff can take two

forms. One is that you will sell more in Japan and hopefully earn bigger profits as well. The other is that, having measured yourself against the best in Japan, you can take these same products and techniques and apply them with even greater effect elsewhere.

Unfortunately, there are not so many examples of *gaishi* taking advantage of their presence in Japan to improve on local products and then sell them abroad, although there is a noteworthy effort to keep up with the Japanese. Still, it is interesting that Proctor & Gamble came out with both an improved detergent and diaper which were used to good effect both in Japan and in the home market.[2] And Xerox used the experience gained with smaller plain paper copiers in Japan to help in America. This may just be the beginning. With Japan now at the leading edge in many sectors, it should increasingly be subject to the indignities of cloning and me-tooing.

That Little Something Extra

Foreigners have no trouble following this argument. Wherever you are, you have to refine quality, service, etc. They tend to gag at the last item on our earlier list, one they might never have included to start with, connections. The Japanese business community is riddled with connections, many we would consider not only superfluous but cumbersome, and some which would be banned as illegal or at least unethical in other countries. There are countless links between producers and distributors, parent companies and subcontractors, sellers and buyers. Relations exist not only between companies that cooperate but competitors, whether through trade associations or cartels.

If a *gaishi* is going to flourish in Japan, it has to fit in with this pattern in some manner. It must accept that ''minding your own business'' and ''arm's length relations'' are not the rule here. This means that, at the simplest level, there should

be somewhat more socializing, a greater effort to know per-
sonnally those you are dealing with. In Japanese parlance, a
"wet" approach. It also includes participation in activities
of business organizations and even friendly clubs of competing companies. Although you might draw the line at anything that would be regarded as illegal back home.

But there is no reason you cannot go further, as the Japanese
do, with regard to financial participation in companies which
serve you and whose service is particularly important. You
may wish to buy equity in your distributors or subcontractors
just to make sure the relationship becomes a long-standing
one. If not, there is no harm in some gentle persuasion through
financial arrangements. If you do gain the upper hand, it
should be consolidated by placing loyal employees on the
board or in key staff positions.

This may sound a bit strong. But it is the Japanese way.
Close relations are not forged purely by sociability and friendship. You need something more. After all, due to rotation,
there is so much turnover that staff you patiently cultivated
are soon replaced by newcomers. Worse, those in favor of a
continuing relationship may be ousted by opponents in a
management shakeup. Only with effective financial and personnel ties can you be certain the relationship will endure.
And even then you may lose out to others, especially Japanese
companies whose ties are firmer.

There is presently much talk about getting Japanese politicians and retired officials to lobby for foreign firms. Apparently, some progress is actually being made and a few big
names were signed up. But that is easier said than done for,
once having sided with *gaijin,* these figures tend to lose credibility. Much more promising is to cultivate better relations
with lower level bureaucrats, those you have to work with
on a regular basis. Don't adopt the same "we don't mix with
government" or "they are just civil servants" attitude as
back home. It could be costly.[3]

Keep Growing

Returning to business more or less as usual, it is worthwhile highlighting one aspect that can contribute greatly to success, namely growth. As every foreign businessman knows, the Japanese place tremendous emphasis on growth. As for the choice between profit and market share, many Westerners and some Asians will not share this preference, although the latter will certainly understand it better. There is no intrinsic reason why a company must continue expanding, especially if the process is costly and risky. So, let us first consider some advantages.

Before all else, it must be remembered that Japan's is still a growing economy. It is not growing as rapidly as before, but it keeps ahead of the average. And, in an expanding economy, any company which does not also expand at least at the same rate is actually shrinking. It is losing market share which could ultimately be fatal. Thus, even if you are not hell bent on growth, you might consider whether growth equivalent to that in your sector should not be integrated in your objectives.

Growth will help you with productivity. You have a given staff, offices, factories, warehouses and so on. If you increase sales, you will be enhancing the productivity of these fixed investments. Higher productivity will ultimately help your bottom line. That is one justification for modest growth that any head office can understand. The folks back home will only question further expansion, expansion that requires more staff, offices, factories, warehouses and so on.

Still, if you are growing yet more rapidly, you can more readily accomplish many of your other goals. With a larger operation, it is much easier to come out with new, improved products, to refine production techniques, to shorten delivery times, etc. Growth, especially among Japanese, also invigorates the staff. Salesmen push ahead more aggressively, managers rally the ranks of *sararimen* and factory workers who, since there may be more overtime or bigger bonuses, are willing to make greater sacrifices.

Growth also ties in with personnel management more intimately if you adopt the Japanese system. If you merely hire and fire, then you can add or discard staff in keeping with production levels. If you bring in new classes of young employees and intend to keep them throughout a career, there must be something for them to do not only now but three decades from now. They should also have legitimate hopes of riding the escalator up. That can only be provided by an expanding operation. Just holding your own is not enough.

This, however, does not mean that you have to succumb to the growth mania that affects many Japanese, where projects are adopted purely for reasons of growth or to keep the staff happy, without considering their merits. Nor do you have to introduce a new model, build a new factory or launch an ambitious advertising campaign just because your competitors do. It is necessary to weigh more soberly than most Japanese managers the pros and cons. You have to determine whether it will yield an acceptable return and, above all, whether your rivals are not all doing the same thing at the same time which could be ruinous.

Moreover, if you want to grow, there are more ways than one. The most obvious is to add new products. There is nothing unusual about that. Yet, as an extension of a foreign company, you may be in a somewhat better position. You may not have to develop these products but simply pick some of those already being sold back home and check whether they can do well in Japan. In fact, given the importance of growth, this should be part of a strategy of starting with one or two especially promising articles and gradually expanding.

Another relatively tame way of growing is to enlarge the distribution network. There are probably dozens of wholesalers and other distributors in your sector and you may just

be working with a few. It would not hurt to add more gradually. Obviously, when adding, you should try to avoid du-
plication by going into new regions or types of outlets.
Meanwhile, the older distributors can be satisfied by letting
them handle some of the new products added to the line. Or,
if you are more ambitious, you might try marketing some of
these products yourself.

A further step, this time more audacious, is to take up local
production. This can be done in various ways. If you already
have a joint venture, the task will be shared with your partner
who doubtlessly has more experience and may just suggest
using one of its existing plants and personnel. That is easier.
But the risk remains that now, in addition to controlling
distribution, your partner will know how to manufacture the
products. If you have your own operation you may still go
into a specific joint venture to manufacture a specific product
but choose another associate for the next, so as to dilute the
risk.

It is certainly more complicated and costly to set up your
own factory from scratch, recruit a completely new staff,
train technicians, managers, etc. This is also very risky. You
will not know from the outset just how big the plant should
be. Too small and it is less productive than those of your
competitors. Too large and you will be stuck with excess
capacity. You may then fall into the usual trap of cutting
prices to boost sales and thereby neglecting profit, which
would not appeal to the head office.

A third alternative, one I have seldom heard but sounds
very constructive, was suggested by Kuniyasu Sakai, an author *and* businessman. That is to tap into the Japanese subcontracting system.

"A foreign company could choose to bypass the big Japanese manufacturer, split up production among a couple of
reliable smaller companies, and avoid the whole problem.
The key to this approach is the basic interests of the small

subcontractor: it doesn't want to compete with you—it wants more orders from you."[4]

The advantages are considerable, some already mentioned. Less risk of being dominated by your partner, less chance of it creating a clone product that ultimately competes against you, yet the ability to have others produce what you need without getting involved in manufacturing yourself. But that is not all. As I noted earlier on, subcontractors tend to be quite efficient, they are much cheaper than large companies and they could become dependent on you. If you do well, they can expand production or you can add more subcontractors. If things do not work out, you can lay them off.

The final step, the consecration as it were, is local research and development. That will really prove to the Japanese business community and your own employees that you are in for the long haul. That is obviously not why you should make the decision. Far better reasons are that Japan now has a large number of trained and experienced research workers and many advanced technologies originate here. If you want to keep ahead, you should take advantage. That is already being done by IBM, DuPont, Eastman Kodak and many of the pharmaceutical firms.

Upgrade Your Operation

Growth can assume another dimension as well. This involves raising your profile in Japan and, while so doing, increasing your commitment and chances of success. The path was already marked out rather clearly when referring to the various points of entry. It is possible to enter at one of the lower and subsequently move up.

The lowest rung, as indicated, is merely to export to Japan whether through a trading company or a smaller importer. At this level, however, you are almost entirely dependent on the agent's ability. There is little means of evaluating how effective a job it is doing. There is not much feedback from the customers. You do not even have that much influence over advertising or pricing. Worst of all, you never know when the agent may replace you with another supplier.

With a representative office, you can at least maintain some degree of control. You can more readily check on the efficiency of distribution and evaluate consumer tastes to determine whether and how to modify any product. You can also get a better feel for pricing, advertising and other forms of promotion. Knowing the market better, you may also encounter alternative distribution channels. You could even replace the trading company or importer and take charge of marketing yourself.

Moving to a joint venture or a wholly owned, full-scale operation is a big step. It is probably best to decide from the outset which it will be since forming a joint venture is complicated and costly. Dissolving one is even more troublesome and, if your old partner is not happy, could leave you with a battered reputation. Worse, the former partner could turn into a competitor. Nonetheless, there has been a definite trend for foreign companies which started out with joint ventures to dissolve them or buy out the Japanese side. This was done by Bayer, Corning and Kodak.

It is only at the level of a joint venture or wholly owned subsidiary that you can seriously think of marketing or manufacturing. Unfortunately, in the former case, your partner—who knows the situation better—is more likely to take the lead and acquire contacts and expertise you would be wise to reserve for yourself. Equally important, your partner will probably control most of the personnel. If the joint venture ever falls apart, you would not be able to salvage much of it.

So, if you do expect eventually to go into active marketing and manufacturing, let alone R&D, it may be best to skip the joint venture stage entirely. On the other hand, if it does ease entry, another alternative may be considered. Rather than tying up with a large partner that could dominate you, try a smaller one that you can dominate or one in an unrelated sector. With the former, you might eventually buy into or even take over the partner and, in the latter, a divorce would be smoother. It might also be possible to acquire smaller distributors or subcontractors which have manufactured goods for you.

Acquisitions are not as frequent in Japan. Nor are they easy given the prevalent crossownership and vested interests of existing personnel. But they are not as difficult as before. This is particularly true when it is a friendly takeover, one that occurs between companies which have already been doing business for some time and where there is a proper fit. If the foreign company is known by the target enterprise, and it feels it could benefit from an infusion of capital or know-how, it might be receptive. Indeed, it may well prefer being rescued by a foreign company to being swallowed up by a Japanese rival. That could explain General Motor's holdings in Isuzu and Ford's in Mazda. Other mergers and acquisitions were undertaken by Kodak, Corning Glass, Motorola and Merck.[5]

The ultimate step, although it has been taken by few enough foreign companies, is to create your own group or mini-*keiretsu*. This can go in all three directions, with the parent company controlling suppliers and subcontractors, dominating distributors and even doing business on a reasonably equal footing with a major bank and its related companies. Examples of this are Bayer, BASF, DuPont, Exxon, General Electric and, of course, IBM.[6]

What If It Doesn't Work Out?

The literature on foreign companies operating in Japan is rather one-sided. It tends to stress the successes which were apparently achieved by using the tried-and-true methods espoused by the writer.[7] There were failures, it is admitted, but that is because the *gaishi* did not do things right. It did not adapt its products, it did not refine quality, it did not meet deadlines, it could not cooperate with Japanese distributors or joint venture partners and so on. The solution, the only one most "experts" can conceive of, is to try harder because, as we all know, Japan is a tough market and it takes time.

This whole patter is wrong. First of all, there are more failures than are generally conceded. These failures include not only companies which have publicly given up and pulled out. There are others which still function but cannot cover their costs or even generate enough business to keep their employees busy. Many show reasonable profits. But, if they are losing market share at the same time, their future is hardly assured. Others are comfortable joint ventures where the Japanese partner runs the personnel, sales and production and may ultimately find that a foreign partner is a drag.

No matter how unpleasant it may be, many of the *gaishi* would be wise to admit their failure or at least lack of convincing success. They should then consider which measures can be taken to turn the venture around. In some cases, this may involve rather dramatic reforms, in others, relatively minor changes. What they do will depend very heavily on where the fault lies.

Most often it is simply assumed that the foreign side must be doing something wrong. This may well be. The man sent out by the head office may not be good in a foreign setting, especially the Japanese one. He may not relate well to the personnel or grasp the tricky marketing situation. He may find it hard to cooperate and prefer giving orders. Even more simply, the product chosen to spearhead the entry may have been the wrong one. It sold well in New York, or London, or Singapore, but bombed in Japan, at any rate in its present form.

On the other hand, it may not be the fault of the foreign

company but those it is working with in Japan. This sort of possibility arises particularly in the case of exporting or licensing. It is entirely possible that the trader, importer or manufacturer is not terribly efficient. It may not have the best distribution network or, even if it is good, it may not be entirely adapted to the needs of your product. In addition, since it tends to do things its own way, it may not truly understand the product's selling points. If it has an interest in other companies which make competing products or, even more insidious, is controlled by them, it may not be very committed to your success.

In joint ventures, there can be similar problems. The Japanese partner may not have as good a distribution network as was assumed and it may not even be manufacturing as efficiently as others. That can happen. More likely is that the parent company has other things to worry about, projects with a higher priority, and it therefore only transferred to your operation some of its less competent or dynamic people and less efficient production facilities. More serious, once again, it may now be in a position where it could produce and sell a comparable product and would secretly like to see the joint venture collapse.

So, why not consider a failure in Japan as cooly and objectively as anywhere else? Just because you feel you must succeed and just because the media will jump on any setback does not mean you have to continue along the same path. There is no reason you cannot recall the expatriate boss or even depose a Japanese CEO. You could very well try other distributors or even completely different channels. If things are bad enough, you may want to dissolve a joint venture and go out on your own. Less often, but still a possibility, you may find that creating a wholly owned subsidiary was too ambitious and you are better off with a local partner who knows the market and has more clout.

There are drawbacks to all of these solutions. You may

have to revamp your whole distribution and even production machinery, you may make enemies with former employees who can have allies within the existing staff, you will certainly anger the distributors, which should not be done lightly. Your former joint venture partner will not be very happy and it can influence others in the group or more broadly. You may end up with a bad reputation. This is all negative, very negative. But it is probably less harmful than preserving an operation that is a failure and continues being a burden on the company and source of ridicule in the Japanese business community.

If worse comes to worst, you may even have to take a decision that is anathema to most consultants . . . withdraw from Japan. That is the clearest admission of failure and it is particularly embarrassing in Japan where your fellow *gaijin* will excoriate you and Japanese companies will claim you have proven that foreigners cannot hack it. Yet, no matter how painful the decision, it is better to fail and leave than to fail and stay. You will look less ridiculous and perhaps gradually be forgotten.

Is a comeback possible? Can you revamp, retrench or return? For some odd reason, the consensus is that you cannot. That seems to be based largely on theory and cultural considerations. In practice, companies have failed the first time and yet succeeded the second time around. They seriously considered their weaknesses, plotted a more intelligent strategy and made some of the changes mentioned, like trying other personnel, products, distributors, partners or going it alone. They usually also put greater manpower and finance into the new effort and gave success in Japan a higher priority.

There are examples of this. A major reversal in fortune came for automakers in general as duties and NTBs were eliminated, but also as they switched from use of importers to opening their own dealerships, BMW being the most prominent. General Foods, on the other hand, having failed to expand its market share for instant coffee alone, became more effective in a tie-up with Ajinomoto. Kodak, an old-timer, only really began clicking over recent years when it gave Japan the priority it merited. Nothing is more instructive than the already cited experience of Procter & Gamble, whose initial successes with both detergents and diapers were undermined by Japanese clones, which it then improved upon.

Actually, comebacks and turnarounds have been occurring with increasing frequency as the artificial barriers come down and *gaishi* figure out how the market works. This makes any hard-and-fast rules rather questionable. It is a matter of trying, and trying, and trying again until you find the right combination to succeed. If I am not mistaken, that principle applies in most countries, and not only Japan. The only difference is that here you have to try a bit harder.

NOTES

1. Kang, op. cit, p. 66.
2. On the Procter & Gamble story, see Huddleston, op. cit., pp. 185–92.
3. In some ways this ties up with Kang's third, and final, phase of becoming a "semi-insider." For more on what this entails and how it can be achieved, see Kang, op. cit., pp. 46–9 and 67–8.
4. For revealing insight into Japanese manufacturing, and what it signifies for foreign businessmen, see Kuniyasu Sakai, "The Feudal World of Japanese Manufacturing," *Harvard Business Review*, November– December 1990, pp. 38–49.
5. On mergers and acquisitions, see Kanji Ishizumi, *Acquiring Japanese Companies*, and Carl W. Kester, *Japanese Takeovers*.
6. See Dodwell, *Industrial Groupings in Japan*, 1989, pp. 277–300.
7. On the "success" of foreign companies in Japan, to be taken with an extra dose of salt, see Robert C. Christopher, op. cit. On some failures, see James C. Abegglen and George Stalk, Jr., *Kaisha*, pp. 214–41.

Bibliography

Books

Abegglen, James C., *The Strategy of Japanese Business,* Cambridge, Ballinger, 1984.

———, and Stalk, Jr., George, *Kaisha, The Japanese Corporation,* New York, Basic Books, 1985.

Alston, Jon P., *The Intelligent Businessman's Guide to Japan,* Rutland and Tokyo, Tuttle, 1990.

American Chamber of Commerce in Japan, *Living in Japan,* Tokyo, updated periodically.

Ballon, Robert J., and Tomita, Iwao, *The Financial Behavior of Japanese Corporations,* Tokyo and New York, Kodansha International, 1988.

Batzer, Erich, and Laumer, Helmut, *Marketing Strategies and Distribution Channels for Foreign Companies in Japan,* Boulder, Westview, 1989.

British Chamber of Commerce in Japan, *Japan Posting, Preparing to Live in Japan,* Tokyo, 1990.

Christopher, Robert C., *Second To None: American Companies in Japan,* New York, Crown, 1986.

Czinkota, Michael, and Woronoff, Jon, *Unlocking Japan's Markets: Seizing Marketing and Distribution Opportunities in Today's Japan,* Chicago, Probus, 1991.

De Mente, Boye, *How To Do Business With The Japanese,* Chicago, NTC Publishing, 1987.

Eli, Max, *Japan, Inc.: Global Strategies of Japanese Trading Corporations,* Chicago, Probus, 1991.

Fields, George, *Gucci on the Ginza: Japan's New Consumer Generation,* Tokyo and New York, Kodansha International, 1989.

Graham, John L., and Sano, Yoshihiro, *Smart Bargaining, Doing Business with the Japanese,* New York, Harper Business, 1989.

Hall, Edward T., and Hall, Mildred Reed, *Hidden Differences: Doing Business with the Japanese,* Garden City, Anchor Press, 1987.

166

Hamada, Tomoko, *American Enterprise in Japan*, Albany, SUNY, Press, 1991.

Hasegawa, Keitaro, *Japanese-Style Management, An Insider's Analysis*, Tokyo and New York, Kodansha International, 1986.

Hayashi, Shuji, *Culture and Management in Japan*, Tokyo, University of Tokyo Press, 1988.

Huddleston, Jr., Jackson N., *Gaijin Kaisha, Running A Foreign Business in Japan*, Armonk, M.E. Sharpe, 1990.

Imai, Masaaki, *Kaizen, The Key To Japan's Competitive Success*, New York, McGraw-Hill, 1986.

Ishizumi, Kanji, *Acquiring Japanese Companies, Mergers and Acquisitions in the Japanese Market*, Cambridge, Basil Blackwell, 1988.

Kang, T.W., *Gaishi, The Foreign Company in Japan*, New York, Basic Books, 1990.

Kester, W. Carl, *Japanese Takeovers, The Global Contest for Corporate Control*, Boston, Harvard Business School, 1990.

Koike, Kazuo, *Understanding Industrial Relations in Modern Japan*, New York, St. Martin's Press, 1988.

Kono, Toyohiro, *Strategy & Structure of Japanese Enterprises*, London, Macmillan, 1984.

Kuboi, Takashi, *Business Practices and Taxation in Japan*, Tokyo, Japan Times, 1989.

Lanier, Alison R., *The Rising Sun on Main Street, Working With the Japanese*, Yardley, International Information Associates, and Tokyo, Yohan, 1990.

Lynn, Leonard H., and McKeown, Timothy J., *Organizing Business, Trade Associations in American and Japan*, Lanham, American Enterprise Institute, 1988.

March, Robert M., *The Japanese Negotiator, Subtlety and Strategy Beyond Western Logic*, Tokyo and New York, Kodansha International, 1988.

Maurer, P. Reed, *Competing in Japan*, Tokyo, Japan Times, 1989.

Metraux, Daniel Michael, *The Japanese Economy And The American Businessman*, Lewiston, Edwin Mellon Press, 1990.

Moran, Robert T., *Getting Your Yen's Worth: How to Negotiate with Japan, Inc.*, Houston, Gulf Publications, 1985.

Morgan, James C., and Morgan, J. Jeffrey, *Cracking The Japanese Market*, New York, Free Press, 1991.

Musashi, Miyamoto, *The Book of Five Rings, The Real Art of Japanese Management*, New York, Bantam, 1982.

Nevins, Thomas J., *Labor Pains and the Gaijin Boss*, Tokyo, Japan Times, 1983.

———, *Taking Charge in Japan*, Tokyo, Japan Times, 1990.

Prestowitz, Jr., Clyde V., *Trading Places, How We Allowed Japan to Take the Lead*, New York, Basic Books, 1988.

Rowland, Diana, *Japanese Business Etiquette,* New York, Warner, 1985.

Tatsuno, Sheridan M., *Created in Japan, From Imitators to World-Class Innovators,* New York, Harper & Row, 1990.

Thian, Helene, *Setting Up & Operating A Business in Japan,* Rutland and Tokyo, Tuttle, 1988.

Toyo Keizai, *Japan Company Handbook,* Tokyo, annual.

Tung, Rosalie L., *Business Negotiations with the Japanese,* Lexington, D.C. Heath, 1984.

Woronoff, Jon, *Japan As—Anything But—Number One,* London, Macmillan, New York, M.E. Sharpe, and Tokyo, Yohan, 1991.

———, *Japanese Targeting: Successes, Failures, Lessons,* London, Macmillan, 1992.

———, *Japan's Wasted Workers,* Chicago, Probus, 1992.

———, *World Trade War,* New York, Praeger, 1983.

Yano Research Center, *Market Share in Japan,* Tokyo, annual.

Zimmerman, Mark, *How To Do Business With The Japanese, A Strategy for Success,* New York, Random House, 1985.

Other Publications

Dodwell Marketing Consultants. All periodically updated.
Direct Marketing in Japan
Industrial Goods Distribution in Japan
Industrial Groupings in Japan
Key Players in the Japanese Electronics Industry
Retail Distribution in Japan
The Structure of the Japanese Auto Parts Industry

Japan External Trade Organization (JETRO). Partial listing.
Access to Japan's Import Market Series
Business Information Series
Japan Trade Directory
JETRO Marketing Series
Manufacturing Technology Guide Series
Standards Information Series
Your Market in Japan Series

Periodicals, Newsletters

Business Tokyo (monthly)
    104 Fifth Avenue, New York, NY 10011
The Nikkei Weekly (weekly)
    1-9-5 Otemachi, Chiyoda-ku, Tokyo 100-66
Tokyo Business Today (monthly)
    Toyo Keizai Inc., 1-2-1 Nihonbashi Hongokucho,
    Chuo-ku, Tokyo 103
Venture Japan (quarterly)
    Asia Pacific Communications, 27 East 61 Street,
    New York, NY 10021

Directory

Embassies

American Embassy
    1-10-5 Akasaka, Minato-ku, Tokyo 107
Australian Embassy
    2-1-14 Mita, Minato-ku, Tokyo 108
British Embassy
    1 Ichibancho, Chiyoda-ku, Tokyo 102
Canadian Embassy
    7-3-38 Akasaka, Minato-ku, Tokyo 107
French Embassy
    4-11-44 Minami-Azabu, Minato-ku, Tokyo 106
German Embassy
    4-5-10 Minami-Azabu, Minato-ku, Tokyo 106

Foreign Chambers

American Chamber of Commerce in Japan
    No. 2 Fukide Bldg., 4-1-21 Toranomon, Minato-ku,
    Tokyo 105
Australian Chamber of Commerce in Japan
    C.P.O. Box 1096, Tokyo 100-91
British Chamber of Commerce in Japan
    No. 16 Kowa Bldg., 1-9-20 Akasaka, Minato-ku,
    Tokyo 106

Canadian Chamber of Commerce in Japan
    Saita Bldg., 2-16-1 Nishi-Azabu, Minato-ku, Tokyo 106
French Chamber of Commerce & Industry in Japan
    Hanzomon-MK Bldg., 1-8-1 Kojimachi, Chiyoda-ku,
    Tokyo 102
German Chamber of Commerce & Industry in Japan
    Akasaka Tokyu Bldg., 2-14-3 Nagata-cho, Chiyoda-ku,
    Tokyo 100
Italian Chamber of Commerce in Japan
    No. 25 Mori Bldg., 1-4-30 Roppongi, Minato-ku,
    Tokyo 106
Swiss Chamber of Commerce & Industry in Japan
    CS-Tower Bldg., 1-11-30 Akasaka, Minato-ku,
    Tokyo 107

Japanese Organizations

Japan Chamber of Commerce & Industry
    Tosho Bldg., 3-2-2 Marunouchi, Chiyoda-ku,
    Tokyo 100
Japan External Trade Organization (JETRO)
    2-5 Toranomon 2-chome, Minato-ku, Tokyo 105
JETRO, London
    Leconfield House, Curzon Street, London W1Y 7FB
JETRO, New York
    1221 Avenue of the Americas, New York, NY 10020
Japan Federation of Economic Organizations (Keidanren)
    1-9-4 Otemachi, Chiyoda-ku, Tokyo 100
Manufactured Imports Promotion Organization (MIPRO)
    World Import Mart Bldg., 3-1-3 Higashi-Ikebukuro,
    Toshima-ku, Tokyo 170
Ministry of International Trade & Industry (MITI)
    1-3-1 Kasumigaseki, Chiyoda-ku, Tokyo 100

Other

Dodwell Marketing Consultants
Kowa Bldg. No. 35, 1-14-14 Akasaka, Minato-ku,
Tokyo 107
Japan Export Information Center
Room 2324, U.S. Department of Commerce,
Washington, DC 20230

Index

Books by Jon Woronoff

JAPAN: THE COMING ECONOMIC CRISIS

JAPAN: THE COMING SOCIAL CRISIS

JAPAN'S WASTED WORKERS

WORLD TRADE WAR

JAPAN'S COMMERCIAL EMPIRE

THE JAPAN SYNDROME

ASIA'S "MIRACLE" ECONOMIES

POLITICS, THE JAPANESE WAY

JAPAN AS—ANYTHING BUT—NUMBER ONE

UNLOCKING JAPAN'S MARKETS

JAPANESE TARGETING